C. PAUL STOCKER

DAVID NEAL KELLER

C. PAUL STOCKER

HIS LIFE AND LEGACY

OHIO UNIVERSITY PRESS · ATHENS

© Copyright 1991 by Ohio University Press

Printed in the United States of America

All rights reserved

Ohio University Press books are printed
on acid-free paper ∞

Keller, David Neal.
C. Paul Stocker : his life and legacy / by David Neal Keller.
p.   cm.
ISBN 0-8214-0973-5
1. Stocker, C. Paul (Closman Paul), 1904-1978.   2. Electric engineers—
United States—Biography.   3. Telephone supplies industry—
United States—Biography.   I. Title.
TK6143.S76K45   1990   621.3′092—dc20   [B]   90-35925

Designed by Laury A. Egan

CONTENTS

PREFACE

Compiling information about a remarkable man, his company, his family, and his wide variety of civic, philanthropic, and educational pursuits requires the cooperation of many persons. It is impossible to list all the men and women who submitted to lengthy interviews and, in some instances, correspondence to reflect on the life and accomplishments of Paul Stocker. It was fortunate that his brother Doyle kept records of early family life. Beth Stocker and all members of her family were most generous of their time, particularly considering the modesty they shared with Paul. Special gratitude also goes to Ben Norton, who coordinated communication with the family and the company; former Stocker colleagues Martin Huge, Al Pfaff, Rob Stephenson, Dick McMillan, Jim Goodell, Walter Krok, Frank Borer, Vic Ritter, Charles Ramaley, and many others; Ross Lindsey of Dennison, Ohio; Irving Hopkins of Basking Ridge, New Jersey; Robin Champagne of St. Petersburg, Florida; Ohio University Director of Information Peggy Black; Ohio University Dean of Engineering and Technology T. Richard Robe and former deans E. J. Taylor and Richard Mayer; Ohio University President Charles J. Ping and former presidents John C. Baker and Vernon R. Alden; Photographer Al Pelton, and many other employees of the Lorain Products Division of Reliance Comm/Tec who provided interviews and helped gather materials; the division and its parent company for offering access to files; Peg Chronister, curator of the Museum of Independent Telephony in Abilene, Kansas; Dr. Omar L. Olson, executive director of the Ohio Technical and Community College Association and former president of Lorain County Community College; LCCC Development Officer Robert Kirkpatrick; *Lorain Journal* columnist Jim Mahoney; and my wife, Marian, who provided valuable assistance throughout the project. Finally, I would like to acknowledge the foresight of Paul Stocker himself, who on several occasions wrote detailed reports on company activities, explaining, "If these are kept and filed, they may be of historical interest at some future date."

David Neal Keller

C. PAUL STOCKER

ways contribute directly to social fulfillment. C. Paul Stocker was one of those persons.

Foremost among the inspirational legacies of Paul Stocker is the assurance that financial success can be accompanied by a deep concern for the welfare of others. Wealth never was his primary goal, even though he dreaded being poor. He was modest and genuinely caring to the extent that an honest characterization of his life runs the danger of appearing effusive. He shunned ostentation and was almost embarrassed to receive credit for abundant generosity to his alma mater, myriad other educational and civic organizations, and individuals.

An unmistakable measure of Paul Stocker's stature became evident when nearly all past and present Lorain Products employees who were interviewed during research for this book emphasized what they considered two major qualities of their former employer: He knew the name of every employee, and despite the cyclical nature of the business, he never laid off one person for economic reasons while he was owner and chief executive officer of the company.

PROLOGUE

History is recorded primarily through highlights of wars, industrial developments, and economic crises. Social, religious, and political issues may share, even dominate our day-to-day passions, but few withstand the erosion of time. In the end, textbooks hopscotch through the years, designating eras by celebrated battles, revolutionary inventions, and serious financial depressions.

Consequently, we become well informed on the personal accomplishments of great generals, inventors, and tycoons. Even U. S. presidents, on the other hand, are linked more closely to armed conflicts or economic circumstances of their terms than to their performances in office, their degree of long-term notoriety often depending on the magnitude of associated events. Abraham Lincoln, Woodrow Wilson, and Franklin Roosevelt are readily matched with the Civil War and the two world wars; Herbert Hoover with the stock market crash leading to the Great Depression. But who was president during the Spanish-American War, or even the Korean War? To whose administrations do we attribute non-catastrophic economic upswings and slides?

A seemingly vital premise can become vacuous by failing history's test of feasibility. Exit bomb shelters and paper dresses. Names like Franklin, Edison, Ford, and Bell meanwhile remain exalted because their ideas receive lasting high marks; the products they introduced continue to touch nearly every world citizen in some way.

It is this influence on people's lives that leaves a testament worthy of historical preservation. But the deed need not be attended by fanfare. Without the flamboyance of a Thomas Edison or the single-mindedness of a Henry Ford, many Americans quietly help advance knowledge and in other

ONE

FAMILY INFLUENCES

As America entered the twentieth century, rapid transitions in agriculture and industry generated an outpouring of optimism, tempered somewhat with the bewilderment of sudden change. Railroads had been expanding the nation's flourishing business activities westward since the Civil War. Electric power, although still in its infancy, was altering the nature of factories, homes, and urban transportation. Steel mills with insatiable appetites for iron ore and coal set new records of production and mining that led the way in making American industrial output the largest in the world. Less than twenty-five years after having been introduced as a novelty at America's 1876 centennial, the telephone had become an indispensible commodity, with conversations reaching all the way from New York to Chicago. Automobiles, although not representing a separate industry in the 1900 census, enjoyed widespread popularity.

A series of innovations in agricultural machinery had enabled the number of farms and tilled acreage to double in three decades. This vast expansion substantially lowered the price of farm products, creating a rash of foreclosures and a resulting shift from ownership to tenancy. The plight of small farmers, however, made but a small dent in the overall armor of prosperity that led President McKinley to an easy reelection victory over William Jennings Bryant on a platform stressing the "full dinner pail" years of his previous administration.

In several ways, Tuscarawas County in eastern Ohio represented a microcosm of the nation's economic configuration. The tobacco, wheat, and corn blanketing its rolling hills since pioneer days nurtured an early prosperity, boosted further when the Ohio and Erie Canal passed within its boundaries. The canal's location in a watershed dividing the drainage between Lake Erie and the Ohio River led to the gradual replacement of rich loam with clay washing in from surrounding hills and eventually eliminated tobacco as a feasible crop; but the slack was taken up temporarily by an increase in cereal grain production.

The emergence of such revolutionary machinery as large gang plows, disc harrows, and giant combine harvesters, perfectly adapted to the flat expanse of northwestern Ohio and the Great Plains, but unsuited to traversing the Tuscarawas County hills, gradually made crop farming less competitive. Consequently, by 1900, the county's gentle slopes had become home to herds of cattle, tended primarily by descendants of German and Swiss immigrants who represented both a large percentage of the county's farmers and a heritage of expertise in dairy farming. By organizing successful cooperatives, they captured large shares of markets in Swiss cheese and other milk products.

Meanwhile, the county's clay substructure, which had doomed tobacco farming, became the raw material of a major industry. The new Royal Clay Works quickly became one of the nation's largest manufacturers of sewer pipe (later supplying much of the drain tile used to construct the Panama Canal). Others businesses followed, reaching a total of twenty-seven companies manufacturing tile, bricks, pottery, and other clay products.

Coal mining and railroading were no less important to the economy. More than a million tons of bituminous coal were extracted from dozens of small shaft mines surrounding the Tuscarawas River, which ran diagonally across the county. On opposite banks of a tributary known as the Little Stillwater, the twin cities of Dennison and Uhrichsville, with a combined population of less than 8,000, showed promise of becoming an important industrial complex. Dennison had, in fact, been founded as a railroad center, with workers moving in from Pittsburgh, Cincinnati, and Chicago to lay a network of tracks, construct repair shops, and operate terminals. Uhrichsville, having been founded much earlier (1804), was the established vitrified sewer pipe center of the entire nation. With cities and towns across the country competing to build sewerage systems, the Uhrichsville skyline was described as glowing dramatically with the night fires of numerous kilns.

Among the enterprising area residents was a young stone mason, Closman Reed Stocker, already respected as a man of versatile talents, not the least of which was a seemingly innate instinct for horse trading. That special talent had been honed to a sharp edge by his father, Henry Stocker, who owned a Dennison livery stable, and an older brother, Marshall, who recently had moved to Montana, where he bought wild mustangs and shipped them by rail to dealers in Ohio. Henry Stocker, at six-foot-four, was considerd a giant in his time. Closman, an even six feet tall, was lean and reserved, but Marshall, a stocky five-foot-seven, was described by friends as "rugged and rather untamed." A sister, Golda, was referred to in family documents simply as the "middle child." The children were born in the village of Gayesport, near Zanesville, Ohio, before Henry moved the family to Dennison.

———

When Closman Stocker married Cinderella Crites on the last day of 1902, he abandoned his job as head of a team cutting stones for railroad tunnels to become a tenant farmer. On January 11, 1904 the first of three sons was born to the young couple. They named him Closman Paul Stocker but called him by his middle name to avoid confusion.

Cinderella Crites had been reared in the small town of Tuscarawas, just west of Dennison, where she had played the organ in a Lutheran church and worked as a bookkeeper for a flour mill. Her father had marched with General Sherman's army on its celebrated march to the sea.

Friends knew the young Mrs. Stocker as a friendly, modest woman who loved music and was meticulous in keeping written notes on all the farm's business transactions, making certain each included appropriate dates and accurate figures.

Religion was inbedded in the lives of both Closman and Cinderella Stocker. However, despite his compromising on most things, at the time of their marriage the new husband insisted that his bride transfer allegiance to the Methodist church, in which he was an active layman. He vowed also that their family always would have an abundance of food, something he referred to as "a good table," no matter what else might need to be sacrificed. As a youngster he had experienced severe hunger on many occasions.

The Stockers continued to farm rented land when their other two sons were born, Glenn in 1905 and Doyle in 1909. In 1911, however, they moved into Dennison, where Closman worked with his father at the livery stable for a year. Then they resumed farming, this time obtaining a mortgage for their own home and 163 acres in the Irish Run Valley, three and a half miles east of town.

Many years later, the influences of family and farm life were to become quite evident in the personality of Paul Stocker. Some would be obvious, others more subtle. His insistence on dating memos was to become legend, and businessmen who knew nothing of his boyhood would refer to him as a "skilled horse trader" in negotiating commercial transactions.

Even before his teenage years, young Paul Stocker was fascinated with his father's skill in dealing for horses. It was not unusual to make several trades during a single trip to town and back, and in one particular year the books indicated more profit from horse trading than from farming. A close friend observed that "Closman had only completed one year of high school, but he was an extremely intelligent man, and he was not a person who could be fooled."

When a group of eleven farm families formed a small independent telephone company—a party line with no "central"—Closman Stocker was elected its president. Several years later, the company was absorbed into the Bell System. The education of their sons was a major concern of both parents. Not satisfied with what the boys were learning in a small rural schoolhouse, they paid a dollar a month for each to attend grade school in Dennison. The boys commuted by horse and buggy, which they left at their grandfather's livery stable during the day. At home, the sons were encouraged to read, and the entire family gathered around the organ to sing.

"Mother was a soprano and dad had a great bass voice," Doyle Stocker later recalled. "Dad even sang while he worked, and all three of us picked up that habit." After their voices changed, Paul, Glenn, and Doyle joined a friend in forming a church quartet. Paul had been encouraged by his mother to learn the violin when he was quite young, but other intrigues held higher priorities for him. In desperation, she tried locking him in his room to practice, but finally gave up, admitting she would have to settle for the satisfaction of knowing that at least he enjoyed music.

When their father believed it was time the boys learned to swim, he helped them build a dam on the bend of a nearby creek. As soon as they could demonstrate what he established as proper swimming proficiency, he bought them bathing suits. Their swimming became a source of pride for the trio; few of their friends at school had such facilities available to them, nor even knew how to swim.

"Dad had strong feelings on what he thought we should know, so he worked with us on a lot of things like that," Doyle explained. "He also taught us the value of humor. Everyone who knew him enjoyed his humor, and after he asked the blessing, our meals became pure entertainment. That was every day, because no matter how busy he was, he ate his meals with us."

Behind the humor was a strict set of values and dedication to discipline. Reminiscing many years later in a letter, Paul Stocker told of being warned that a reprimand in school would bring "more of the same" at home. "As a matter of fact, I probably was not paddled more than twice during my school years," he wrote. "It wasn't necessary because the correction applied to the seat of my pants was of such magnitude that I caught on fast and adjusted my actions accordingly."

Halloween was an adventurous time for the three Stocker sons, who looked forward to creating new forms of mischief in nearby Dennison each year. But they always abided by their father's admonition against even the slightest destruction of property. And as they grew older, they all remembered his warning, "If you ever get in jail, remember that I didn't put you there, so I'm not going to get you out." None of the three ever was arrested.

Closman Stocker didn't believe in wasting words. He was patient in hearing opinions, firm in making decisions. When he said something should not be done, no one filed an appeal. Son Doyle could remember only one instance when his father repeated an order:

> We were eating breakfast one day when Paul and Glenn were both gone. Dad told me to go up to a certain field and start to plow. I explained that I had never opened up a field by myself, and didn't know how to do it. Without looking up from his bacon and eggs, he repeated in a quiet voice, "Go up there and start to plow." Somehow I managed to do it, and when he came up later, he just slapped me on the back and smiled. That's how he did things. After a while we boys weren't afraid to try anything.

Episodes recounted through generations of the family mentioned only two instances when Closman Stocker was visibly angry. The first was when the manager of an electric company misrepresented information critical to the farm operation, thereby receiving the nose-to-nose chastisement of Stocker, who let it be known that he could not "abide a person telling a bare-faced lie." The second recipient of his uncurtained wrath was a horse. After the animal jumped over the tongue of a binder when the family was cutting wheat, temper so overcame Stocker that his wife had to restrain him from killing the errant beast. He finally settled for telling the horse, "I'll never put a harness on you again," and trading it as soon as possible.

Although the family was poor, the children never thought about it. The pledge of a full table was inviolate, even to the point of becoming an economic burden. Friends and relatives knew they always would find outstanding food in the home of Cinderella Stocker, who became better known as Aunt Rella. Relatives arrived from Cleveland, Canton, Akron, Barberton, and other cities, not only for weekends, but for entire vacations on the farm. Being "city folk," they were unable to assist on the farm, but all were good at the dinner table. One summer's tally of guests showed from seven to seventeen guests daily for a period of three months. Aunt Rella's family tree alone branched out from eight brothers and sisters.

Pork was a Stocker staple, because Closman raised a lot of hogs. When asked what was saved during butchering, his stock answer was "everything but the squeal." Dennison at that time was a flourishing railroad center, with several hotels and boarding houses filled most of the time. Each day Paul and Glenn Stocker went to town with a wagon, pulled by the family's swiftest Arabian mare, filled several barrels with garbage, and returned home to feed as many as forty hogs. Being young, they often enjoyed testing the speed of their horse, which supposedly had spent an earlier career on racetracks. Having witnessed this rapid return on several occasions, a neighbor who prided himself on also having exceptional horses, pulled alongside the Stocker wagon one day as it was leaving town and attempted to beat the young men home. The race, however, was so one-sided that Paul and Glenn had unhitched their horse by the time the challenger arrived at their barn. Seeing Closman nearby, the neighbor warned, "You had better be careful or those boys will kill that horse." The elder Stocker, who replied simply, "Oh, I don't think you need to worry about that," joined his sons in reminiscing about the "great race" for many years.

Although the Stockers had several dairy cattle, as well as the hogs, crops occupied most of the acreage at that time. Later, however, it evolved into a dairy farm as had many others in the county.

All the farm machinery was horse drawn and secondhand. Because it never was in good working order when purchased, father and sons became adept at making repairs. But there is no evidence that this sparked a mechanical interest in the eldest son, Paul. The family was more prone to attribute that interest to a "natural flair for mechanical and electric devices." Whatever the cause, the effect soon was evidenced by Paul's absorption in *Popular Science, Popular Mechanics*, and similar publications. Before he was out of junior high school he built a "shock machine" that combined friction and a battery to generate small amounts of electricity. To demonstrate how it worked, he had other youngsters stand in a line holding hands; those on the ends grasped rods attached to his contraption while he slowly turned the handle. The machine became an immediate hit among friends, who loved to experience the strange sensation and determine how much "shock " they could withstand.

By the time he reached high school, his pivotal interest had become the automobile. To Paul Stocker it was the quintessence of intrigue. Nothing could be more exciting than to be an auto mechanic, learning the embodiment of this marvelous new vehicle that rapidly was replacing the buggy and streetcar.

With such strong feelings, it is little wonder that Paul always described as one of his fondest memories the day his father bought a Model T Ford. The occasion had special significance for Paul because the new owner didn't know how to drive. Even more wonderful was the discovery that he was in no hurry to learn. For the time being, he preferred to delegate that responsibility to his oldest son. Members of the family noted that Paul never really had to learn driving. He just got into the seat and drove away on the first try, as if he had been doing it for years.

Yet, driving was not enough for a young man intent on

understanding the inner workings of Henry Ford's popular flivver. When his father took the horse-drawn spring wagon to town for the day Paul could not resist the challenge. Slowly and methodically, he completely disassembled the car, spreading the parts out on the grass in front of the barn. He had no doubt that he could reverse the procedure before his father returned from Dennison.

In later years, no one seemed to recall why Closman Stocker chose to rush on that particular day, but those who saw him return early to the farm vividly remembered his look of disbelief at viewing the dissected anatomy of his new Model T. None, of course, remembered the scene better than the youthful would-be mechanic, who admitted being "scared to death, afraid even to look up at dad," before hearing the calm voice of his father say, "Well, son, put it back together, and don't leave out a bolt." With that, Closman Stocker went on about his work.

Avoiding a crisis by successfully reassembling the Ford in no way settled an inquisitive mind. Continuing his varied assortment of scientific reading, Paul was threatened with expulsion from Dennison High School for hypnotizing classmates during lunch breaks in the furnace room. He also dabbled further into electricity and sold *Farm Journal* magazines to earn money for a .22 caliber rifle, but his thoughts veered only rarely from automobile mechanics.

"I could see myself owning a garage and knowing more than anybody else in the whole country about automobile electrical systems and carburetors," he recalled later. "So if I were to own a garage I would need to know about business methods; I would need to know how to type and how to keep books. This is the reason I took a commercial course in high school."

With chores awaiting him at home each afternoon, Stocker did not have time to take part in sports or other after-school activities. When the work was completed, however, he spent nearly every spare moment reading about automobiles and repairing those of his neighbors. "I remember my pride and joy was a book on automobiles I bought for $9.98," he said.

"This investment wiped out my entire capital assets. Up to that time I had managed to save a nickel here, a penny there, until I had $10.00. After this investment, I had two cents left."

Stocker studied all available material on automotive electrical systems and he soon understood everything except how a generator produces electricity. This puzzle bothered him, but he expected to learn it when he studied physics in his senior year. World War I, however, had depleted the ranks of science teachers, and the Dennison physics instructor proved to be a man studying to become a Baptist minister. Greatly disturbed, the aspiring mechanic sought the advice of his father, who took him to see school Superintendent W. H. Angel. The conversation was something Stocker remembered in nearly exact detail through the years:

> After hearing us out, Mr. Angel turned to my father and said, "This boy is never going to learn how the generator generates electricity until he goes to college and takes electrical engineering." Strange as it may seem, this was the first time I had ever heard the term "electrical engineering." After a few more words of appreciation for his time, we left Mr. Angel, and on the way home I said to my dad, "I think I'll go to college and take electrical engineering." My father said, "Son, that's all right with me if you can do it on your own, but as you know, we're poor and we cannot afford to send you to college." I said, "That's all right, I'm going to college."

Despite the family's small income, the farm mortgage had been retired with money received from mining coal during the war. Closman Stocker, assisted by his sons, had dug the coal from hillside deposits on the farm, then hauled it in wagons to railroad cars for shipment to steel mills in Cleveland. Profits earned before the armistice in 1918 ended demand for the coal had been great in comparison with the family's normal income. Yet, with all the proceeds used to "pay off the farm," Doyle Stocker said later, "there was no apparent change in our lives except knowing we owned the land free and clear."

Once he had decided to go to college, Paul became determined to become an engineer rather than an auto mechanic. After considering several schools in the state, he chose Ohio University, which had an established four-year program in electrical engineering.

In the summer of 1921, with only the experience of having assembled a crystal set, Stocker built a radio, not from a kit, but from materials he fashioned into parts, including coils and condensers—everything but the tubes—designing patterns from things he saw in magazines. This was less than a year after KDKA in Pittsburgh had become the first regular commercial broadcasting station to go on the air. He sold the radio to a fellow church member for seventy-five dollars—enough to pay his first year's tuition—then took the train to Athens, where he enrolled in Ohio University. Being the first person in the family to attend college set a precedent. Both his brothers later followed him to Ohio University—Glenn earned a bachelor of arts degree before launching careers in accounting, teaching, and farming, and Doyle attended one year, then went into politics and business. None of the three brothers resembled his father in size—Doyle, at five-foot-nine, was about two inches taller than Paul and Glenn—but all exhibited many of his distinguishing qualities throughout their lives.

Closman Stocker, who learned to drive after his oldest son went to college, farmed the homestead until the early 1940s, when it was taken over by son Glenn. Closman died in 1946 at the age of sixty-five. Cinderella lived to be eighty-two; she died in 1962. During all those years, members of the family visited each other often and were always together at the farm for Thanksgiving.

The impact of tutelage and encouragement from caring parents had an apparent role in molding the adult personality, as well as the career, of Paul Stocker. His upbringing was evident in relationships with the many persons who would come to know and respect him as a friend, colleague, and employer. He never again lived on a farm, but he always described himself as "an Ohio farm boy." His interests reflected those of his parents, albeit on a much broadened scale. Inquisitiveness remained fixed in his nature, leading him to new ideas and global concerns. But in 1921 his thoughts were focused intently on the new knowledge he hoped to acquire from a college education.

TWO

CRESTS AND VALLEYS

Ohio University in 1921 had just hired a new president, Elmer B. Bryan, who was inaugurated soon after the fall semester began. Like other educational institutions across the country, the university was preparing for a rapid growth in response to the unprecedented prosperity of postwar America. Administrators also hoped to correct a condition the new president considered unhealthy, namely that women outnumbered men on the campus. A first step in attracting more males was to be construction of a new gymnasium for men.

Established in 1804 as the first university in the Northwest Territory, Ohio University had advanced in spurts and suffered periodic setbacks corresponding to economic fluctuations. The forested hill country of southeastern Ohio provided a beautiful setting that, along with a small population, created a residential campus atmosphere. Unlike institutions in urban areas of the state, "O.U." had few commuters.

Emphasis in recent years had been placed on liberal arts and preparation for teaching careers, but specialization in engineering was becoming increasingly important. Engineering was not yet recognized as a separate college, however, so when Paul Stocker began his freshman year, his major courses officially were in the Department of Physics and Electrical Engineering. Nevertheless, electrical engineering had grown from a single course in 1890 (just eight years after the nation's first such course was introduced at M.I.T.) to a full curriculum offering the bachelor of science degree.

During his first academic year, freshman Stocker spent

nearly all nonsleeping hours attending classes, studying, waiting on tables at a women's dormitory cafeteria, and working at other part-time jobs. By the middle of the second semester, still without money available from home, the burden became overwhelming. When a job opportunity became available at Timken Roller Bearing Company in Akron that summer, he reluctantly decided to leave school for one year.

For fifteen months, Stocker worked twelve hours a day, seven days a week, taking full advantage of Timken's accelerated schedule to meet customer demands of the booming 1920s. "All I did was work, eat, and sleep," he said later, in recollecting what he considered the most physically strenuous period of his life. But he offered no complaint. By saving what he had earned and resuming his cafeteria job, he was able to reenter the university as a sophomore in the fall of 1923.

A good student who became recognized as an innovator, Stocker never wavered from his resolve to become an electrical engineer. With the help of a friend majoring in psychology, he gained a degree of interdepartmental notoriety by inventing a lie detector that was tested on faculty members as well as students, and determined to be functional. Except for wrestling, a club sport just before gaining varsity status, he took part in few activities not associated with his engineering major. Time was too precious for someone still working his way through college.

Stocker mentioned only two lasting regrets from his four-year college experience. One was that the combination of his work schedule and course requirements made it impossible to take enough courses in the humanities to satisfy his special interests in English and American literature. The other was missing musical performances, which at that time had admission charges for students.

Neither of these disappointments diminished in any way the deep satisfaction he always expressed for his education, nor the warm feeling of loyalty he maintained, and later demonstrated, for Ohio University. Instead, they left an impression of what might be done someday for others striving to gain the benefits of education.

Prior to Commencement, a representative from Bell Laboratories, headquartered in New York City, interviewed graduating seniors at Ohio University. His report highly recommended hiring Stocker, and in June 1926, an exhilarated neophyte engineer who had grown up on a small Ohio farm headed for the nation's largest city. Most important, he would be working with an organization specializing in experimentation.

––––––

Under the leadership of its brash new mayor, James J. "Jimmy" Walker, New York City in 1926 was experiencing a colossal program of revitalization that prompted a *Times* writer to report, "The physical aspects of Manhattan change daily . . . the city of yesterday merges fast into the New York of tomorrow and the present is overshadowed by greater changes to come." Construction was underway on a shoreline thoroughfare, several elevated highways, and additional subways. Tenements and former mansions alike were being razed to make room for large apartment buildings. Plans were completed for construction of a vehicular tunnel to Jersey City, a tri-borough bridge linking Manhattan with Queens and the Bronx, a parkway system to Long Island, and the world's longest suspension bridge, which would cross the Hudson River to New Jersey. (Unnamed at that time, the George Washington Bridge was started in 1927 and opened four years later.) Mayor Walker went so far as to predict the end of slums and conversion of the Harlem River into another River Seine.

New plazas and centers were being developed in the city's five boroughs, and the West Side of Manhattan was about to enter the initial phase of its first major development in fifty years. New theaters and galleries were either being started or planned (as were a number of speakeasies not mentioned in official reports).

City planners seemed determined to disprove Henry Ford's well-publicized prediction that large cities such as New York would shrink as populations shifted to new small communities clustered around individual factories. The mayor insisted that his metropolis, in addition to being the commercial and financial capital of the Western Hemisphere, would continue to be the foremost manufacturing city in the United States and a leader in scientific research. One of its most recent examples was the research facility operated by the American Telephone & Telegraph Company in midtown Manhattan.

———

Bell Telephone Company, organized just two years after the famous inventor received what many considered "the most valuable single patent ever issued" on March 3, 1876, was the forerunner of a spreading corporate system that eventually dominated the telephone industry. Early competition from the Western Union Telegraph Company (which earlier had scoffed at the telephone as being a toy) was eliminated through litigation involving patent infringements. At the same time, the Western Electric Manufacturing Company of Chicago, which had produced telephone equipment for Western Union, became licensed to provide the same work for the Bell organization. Following a chain of reorganizations and name changes, Western Electric became the manufacturing unit of the American Bell Telephone Company, a Massachusetts corporation.

When the Massachusetts Legislature refused to authorize capitalization for wide extensions of long-distance lines, a holding company named American Telephone and Telegraph was formed and chartered in New York. It owned and operated long-distance lines and functioned as a centralized administrative unit for the entire system, which included Bell as the operating arm, Western Electric as the manufacturer.

Although the organization's research programs had descended directly from the early Boston laboratories of Alexander Graham Bell, it was not until the 1920s that a move was made to consolidate such efforts into a separate centralized unit. Bell Telephone Laboratories, Inc., was created in 1925 to serve both the Western Electric Company and the twenty-five Bell System operating companies of AT&T. *The Telephone Engineer*, in its February 1925 edition, offered one of several reports on the event:

Extensions of laboratory facilities for the scientists and engineers of the new Bell Telephone Laboratories, Inc., are already underway. Laboratory space in the form of a new building covering almost a quarter of a city block will be added to the 400,000 square feet at present in service in the group of buildings at 463 West Street, New York City. At the date of incorporation, the personnel numbered approximately 3,600, of whom about 2,000 are members of the technical staff, made up of engineers, physicists, chemists, metallurgists, and experts in various fields of technical endeavor.

The formation of Bell Telephone Laboratories provides an individual organization, the whole activities of which may be more efficiently devoted to the furtherance of research, development, and engineering investigations along the line in which the parent companies have already made such remarkable progress. Its formation is an indication of the estimate which these companies place upon the importance of properly organized research and is a promise of continuous service to the public, to the communication art, and to the progress of science.

The new facility was completed shortly before Paul Stocker arrived to take his place as a junior member of the engineering research group. Heeding the advice of a company representative, he soon moved into a rooming house on 84th Street near Central Park, commuting to his job by subway. The landlady, Mrs. Hopkins, kept her door partially ajar so she could hear what was happening among the young men who lived there, but she was pleasant and well liked and sometimes cooked a meal for the entire group. Most often, however, they ate at small restaurants in the area.

Stocker's work in the laboratory offered the precise opportunity he had sought. After a period under careful supervision, he was permitted to work independently on designated engineering projects and sometimes on those of his own choosing. "Paul moved rapidly into the creative end of things," recalled Irving Hopkins, a colleague recruited at M.I.T. "He was very bright, and could express his thoughts extremely well, always in a soft voice. Being somewhat quiet didn't mean he didn't like to have a good time, though. He had a great sense of humor, and he liked to go out on the town, especially to the theaters."

Hopkins, who regularly had to explain that he was not related to the landlady, was Stocker's roommate at the house on 84th Street, which became home to other young Bell Lab engineers as well. Another close friend was Thomas L. Dimond, a former Iowa farm boy who had received his engineering degree at the University of Iowa. Stocker and Dimond had arrived on the same day to begin their jobs at Bell Labs. Dimond did not live at the same rooming house, but he was a frequent visitor there, and joined the others in social activities. "We all were involved in a variety of experimental projects, but we rarely talked about our work outside the lab," Hopkins said.

One of the things Stocker did mention briefly was his idea for a static frequency converter. Hopkins remembered that his friend "tried to pursue it at the lab, but no one there was interested." They were interested in other things he was doing, however, and after a few years he was moved into a position of greater responsibility as development engineer in a more advanced research department. Ironically, it was that promotion that later cost him his job, yet led to much greater engineering success than he could have achieved with Bell. In the meantime, however, a more important matter was primary in his mind.

Anne Elizabeth Kilpatrick was born in Minnesota, where her father taught in a school for the deaf. Recognized as proficient in what then was a highly specialized area of education—public schools did not enroll hearing-impaired children at that time—Walter Kilpatrick accepted increasingly better offers that took the family to Connecticut, New Jersey, and Washington state. He served as superintendent of state schools for the deaf in the latter two locations. When minor health problems prompted his doctor to prescribe country living, Kilpatrick retired from teaching and moved with his wife, daughter, and son from the Pacific Northwest to a thirty-acre farm near Delaware, Ohio.

There were strong similarities in the parents of Beth Kilpatrick and Paul Stocker. Walter and his wife, Elizabeth, placed great emphasis on the education of their chidren. With pensions for teachers not yet established, the family had little money; they lived on farm earnings that came primarily from raising chickens. Nevertheless, when their daughter graduated from high school in 1924, they managed to finance her enrollment at Ohio University, which had been recommended by friends as offering outstanding programs in science, her preferred field of study.

While majoring in biology, Beth Kilpatrick became active in Women's League, the Women's Athletic Association, YWCA, a local sorority that later became a chapter of Phi Mu, and several other groups. After graduation in 1928, she joined the New York City Health Department as a research bacteriologist. Like Paul Stocker, she had acquired her position through a pregraduation interview on campus.

Fortunately, Beth was able to locate a room at a Girls' Club in Manhattan, thereby complying with a parental pronouncement that she could move to New York City only if she were guaranteed a safe place to live. The club had an international atmosphere—young women from several countries lived there while they either worked or attended graduate school at Columbia University—and Beth's first roommate was from Germany.

Beth Kilpatrick never met Paul Stocker at college. One of

her college roommates, Jeannette Brown, however, lived at Howard Hall, where Paul had been a student dishwasher, and remembered him well enough to know he was working at Bell Labs. Realizing her good friend would be alone in the city, Jeannette telephoned Paul, suggesting he might want to get in touch with Beth.

Paul indeed contacted Beth at the Girls' Club, inviting her to dinner and a show. Three months later they became engaged, and when Beth went home for a vacation, Paul joined her long enough to meet her parents and teenage brother, Walter, who was always called Pat.

Paul and Beth were married on August 5, 1930. While the future Mrs. Stocker returned to the home of her parents to make preparations for the wedding, the bridegroom-to-be stayed in New York for a few days, then drove to Ohio in his first automobile, a 1929 Ford Roadster, complete with rumble seat. Irving Hopkins went with him to serve as best man. Jeannette Brown was maid of honor. Beth wore her grandmother's wedding dress for the marriage ceremony, which was performed by her grandfather, a retired minister.

After they were married, the couple moved into an apartment in Lyndhurst, New Jersey. For two years, both Paul and Beth enjoyed the pleasures of excellent jobs and the cultural offerings of metropolitan New York. Paul received a substantial raise, then a departmental transfer to a still higher salary. Economic conditions, however, had steadily worsened following the Black Thursday stock market crash of November 24, 1929. By the beginning of the new decade, it was obvious that optimistic efforts could not fend off disaster.

––––––

The worldwide depression stunned America. Banks closed, wiping out individual and company savings. Unemployment soared to more than ten million by early 1932, and soup kitchens emerged as factories shut down. Farms were abandoned. Homes were lost. Thousands of people aimlessly roamed the countryside, riding in and underneath boxcars, staying in hobo jungles and scouring neighborhoods for handouts. Many who could not tolerate the humiliation simply ended their lives. A tariff bill, aimed at protecting U. S. business, instead helped spread the economic collapse. With no solution in sight, an anticipated early recovery gave way to hopelessness.

A Bell Systems spokesman described the situation as "temporarily catastrophic." The Great Depression, indeed, was the only period in telephone history that showed a decrease in users and traffic. Salaries were cut at first, and when that could not achieve stability, the company resorted to layoffs. Under such circumstances, development engineers were more expendable than operational personnel.

Bell Labs decided to make cutbacks based on seniority within each department. Even though he had spent six years with the total organization, Paul Stocker was a newcomer to his department. As a result, his employment was "terminated with regret" in August 1932. Typical of his objective reasoning, he showed no bitterness and in fact defended the decision to lay off engineers according to departmental rather than company-wide seniority.

No longer able to afford their apartment in Lyndhurst, Paul and Beth Stocker moved to Rutherford, New Jersey, where they obtained what she considered "very nice quarters" on the top story of a private home. The owner of the house lived on the first floor; the second floor was occupied by one of their sons and his family. Although Beth still had her job, her salary was cut to $80 a month, which represented the couple's sole source of steady income.

While searching in vain for employment, the enterprising but unemployed research engineer mixed brief stints at odd jobs—most of which were as difficult to obtain as regular work—with occasional attempts to market products on his own. Most disastrous among the latter was purchasing a truckload of Christmas trees to sell in Manhattan. "I was out there on a corner in Manhattan, nearly freezing, and rapidly finding out that people didn't even have enough money to buy Christmas trees," Stocker said in retrospect. "Then the police arrested me for not having a vendor's license, and I had to pay a fine that I certainly couldn't afford. The experience was like going through a tornado, and I vowed to never again reach such a low point."

A venture that proved to be more successful, though it seemed implausible to others, typified the Stocker ingenuity. Realizing that jigsaw puzzles had become very popular, but no longer affordable, he decided to produce some that could be offered "for rent," using a jigsaw generously provided by his landlord, who had a basement workshop. To assure popularity in such difficult times, they would have to be extraordinary, but he was confident that could be accomplished. Beginning each puzzle by gluing an art reproduction on plywood, he combined shapes of his own design with those of a few recognizable figures, ranging from animals to a naked woman, in extremely intricate patterns that contained from 300 to 800 pieces. All fit perfectly. To maximize the intrigue, he put the pieces of each puzzle in a plain box, identified only by title, with no picture as a guide. As he alone anticipated, customers were willing to rent the puzzles for twenty-five cents each. As they were returned, Stocker carefully put the puzzles together, making certain no piece was missing. Some of them became prized possessions of the Stocker family.

Despite such inventiveness and his skill in woodworking (which became his favorite hobby), Stocker's scientific precision did not adapt well to cooking. When he decided to assist his working wife in the kitchen, some of the results created what she smilingly remembered as a touch of humor in times of hardship. The most memorable occasion was his decision to prepare a special roast beef dinner before she returned from the city. Reading that he should use garlic, he proceeded to cut a large bulb of the potent herb into small pieces, which he inserted into a perfectly symmetric pattern of punctures around the roast. "He was proud of that roast when he took it out of the oven, and saw that it was beautifully cooked," she said. "Unfortunately, it exceeded the limit of human consumption, so we gave it to the dog, who also refused to eat it."

While preparing another surprise dinner, he followed

directions to put "cold" potatoes into the oven for "au gratin" preparation by dutifully soaking them in ice water. As the couple ate slightly warm raw potatoes, his wife explained that the recipe referred to cold *cooked* potatoes. This, along with the roast beef disaster, was interpreted by Stocker as "an obvious need for neophyte cook books; you can't find anything for a beginner." Had he not been absorbed in other creative matters at the time, he very well might have conducted appropriate research and provided such a publication.

Still interested in automobiles, he invented an oil level indicator that fit on the dashboard. Cars in the 1930s consumed a great deal of oil, and it was important to know how much remained during a long drive. Frequent stops to use a dip stick were annoying, so the new instrument seemed feasible, particularly when Stocker was able to produce it very inexpensively. When he tried to sell the instrument, however, he was shocked to discover that most automotive accessory merchants were uninterested and that the few who did react favorably intended such a high markup for retail sales that the product would have little chance in the depressed marketplace. Other inventions with seemingly important uses, most of them for automobiles, brought similar responses, temporary discouragement, and finally a decision that was to change Stocker's life.

Instead of spending time creating and perfecting new products, then trying to market them, he reasoned, why not reverse the process? With new enthusiasm, Stocker developed a list of a dozen products he felt certain he could invent, then wrote a sales letter extolling the characteristics and advantages of each device. One of them was an item he described as "a new and improved telephone ringing machine without moving parts," the idea he once had suggested to Bell Lab colleagues.

Stocker explained that his plan to build a frequency reducer was based on a discovery made by a Frenchman, Jean Fallou, an electrical engineer with the General Electric Company of France:

Fallou observed a submultiple frequency flowing in a power cable in France. He discovered that this unusual condition was set up by a transient [a temporary oscillation due to a sudden change of voltage or load] in an underground cable feeding a power transformer. Fallou found that the cable capacity and saturation of the power transformer were necessary conditions for a sustained oscillation at the submultiple frequency. He patented a method of starting the oscillation in U. S. patent 1,633,481.

The original idea was to use the Fallou circuit without modification to generate ringing current. The idea was good but it didn't work. Like so many discoveries, it required additional work and invention to make a commercial ringing generator.

Letters describing the intended invention were sent to companies listed in the Thomas Register, a compilation of American manufacturers and products. Although many of those contacted later became good customers, only one letter of interest was received at the time. That letter was from Fred J. Heavens, president of Telkor, Inc. of Elyria, Ohio, who wrote that he would like to see the operating model. In keeping with his new policy, of course, Paul Stocker had not yet built such a prototype.

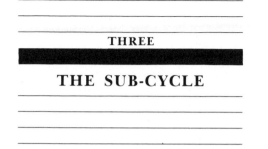

THREE

THE SUB-CYCLE

As an engineer and inventor, Paul Stocker ordinarily adhered to a philosophy of substantiating suppositions with facts. He demanded it of himself and others. Yet, he always was mystified by an unexplainable incident that he insisted took place at the depth of the Depression.

Walking to the interurban station from a library where he had been gathering information on the most recent advancements in circuitry, Stocker saw a large crowd in front of an empty store. When he stopped to investigate, he noticed that a circus barker was enticing onlookers to have his companion, "an old, shriveled Hindu fortuneteller," let them know whether they would find jobs, lose their homes, or in other ways be affected by their problems. Most could not afford the prognostication price of twenty-five cents, so the group soon began to disperse, Stocker among them. Suddenly, however, the fortuneteller shouted, "There is a young engineer working on an invention, and if he will stay, I will talk to him." Astonished at what he had heard, Stocker was "forced by curiosity to stay," although he explained to the barker that he had only twenty-five cents, all of which was needed for his fare to New Jersey. The barker, in turn, started to send him on his way, but the woman was insistent. "You stay here," she said, putting her hands on his head, "I have some things to tell you, and there will be no charge."

What she told him remained so vivid in Stocker's mind that he could, and often did repeat it nearly word for word: "You are working on a patent concerning circuitry. You are going to obtain your patent, but you also will have to buy a foreign patent. Then you will move to the midwestern part of the United States, where you will start a company and eventually become successful and rich."

More than fifty years later, former colleagues said Stocker had repeated the story frequently during his illustrious career, usually at times when the company faced adversity. "If anyone else had told it, I would have thought he was making it up," said a man who himself became president of the company, "but there is not a chance in the world Paul Stocker would have done that."

From the day he received the encouraging letter from Fred Heavens, Stocker channeled all experimentation into perfecting the "ringing machine." His laboratory was the basement workshop, again made available by his landlord. An old card table was converted into a workbench, where he assembled a progression of models, each an attempt to correct flaws in its predecessor. Using copper wire taken from discarded equipment in junk piles, he wound dozens of coils. When one didn't work, he unwound it and used the same wire to try again. Used condensers (now called capacitors) and transformers sometimes were obtained from electrical equipment dealers or made from pieces of scrap metal. Tooling equipment used to fashion parts for the ringing machine likewise was made from materials discarded by machine shops and manufacturing firms. Each time he encountered a new obstacle, Stocker returned to the library to read everything he could find on the properties of various metals and developments in electrical engineering. He also maintained contacts with friends at Bell Laboratories. Both Tom Dimond and Irving Hopkins had survived the layoffs, the latter explaining that he had escaped such a fate "by just a whisker."

Under obvious pressure to provide a demonstration for Fred Heavens, Stocker agreed to visit Telkor as the first stop on a trip he and Beth planned to the homes of their parents, even though work had barely begun on his invention.

Arriving at Telkor's Elyria headquarters early on the appointed day, Stocker encountered a middle-aged man, somewhat shorter than his own five feet, seven inches, friendly, outgoing, and bubbling with nervous energy. One of the initial points of business was the assurance of Fred Heavens that interest in the proposed ringing machine was personal. It did not represent a company consensus. This came as no surprise, because that feeling had been expressed informally in correspondence. Telkor, in fact, marketed a similar product of its own, known as the Telering.

Electric current to ring telephone bells at that time was produced by motor-driven generators, which had replaced the earlier hand-cranked magnetos, except on extremely small exchanges and rural party lines. These ringing generators were operated either with rotating equipment, driven by AC current from commercial power lines, or vibrating reed interrupters converting the power to DC. Both created innumerable problems. Vibrators tended to arc, and their speeds varied with changing conditions. Rotating equipment was expensive to operate and required excessive maintenance.

The advantage Stocker's design offered over Telering and other ringing devices was that no moving parts were used to alter the frequency. A static converter, Stocker's proposed machine reduced sixty-cycle input to twenty-cycle output without the use of vibrating or rotating elements. Rather, the frequency was based on an oscillating circuit in which the tuning inductance could be saturated, thus eliminating equipment fatigue that caused the frequent frustration of breakdowns in telephone exchanges. The critical question was whether the idea would work. Stocker was confident, Heavens skeptical but willing to witness the long-sought demonstration.

Borrowing transformers and condensers from the Telkor laboratory, the inventor began to assemble a sample ringing machine. After two fruitless hours, Heavens left, assuring

Stocker he was free to continue the job. During the remainder of that day and all of the following day, Stocker struggled to prove the workability of his invention, but, in his own words, "I couldn't get a jingle out of it." When he departed, it was with the Telkor president's less-than-encouraging admonition to "let me know if you ever get that thing to work."

Back in his New Jersey "laboratory" after completing the visits to Ohio, Stocker resumed his unyielding search for answers. One major problem was determining how well his machine was responding to improvements. At Bell Labs he would have used an oscillograph (forerunner of the oscilloscope). For a man working alone at a card table in his landlord's basement, however, the cost of such an instrument was prohibitive.

Only one choice remained; using old motors, scrap parts, and mirrors glued to a wheel, Stocker constructed an oscillograph. Beams of light thrown onto a rotating mirror attached to a shaft were viewed through a lens, and a homemade galvanometer connected to an electric circuit provided oscillation. Most of the materials were obtained from junkyards.

Except for outings shared with his wife and their friends, Stocker rarely took time off from work. Even away from the project, it was difficult to divert his thinking from the job. The longest he spent away from the workshop was three days in Washington, D.C., thoroughly searching patent records to make certain no one else had developed a similar product. Beth, meanwhile, continued to work for the Health Department.

As Stocker improved the method of producing acceptable oscillations, other formidable problems appeared. The antiquated capacitors blew up under the voltage necessary for operation. Then he discovered the transformer he was using to step up voltage was becoming saturated prematurely. Undaunted, he made adjustments until the completed invention was ready for a final demonstration. This time the results were spectacular. The ringing machine with no moving parts was ready for production.

Two years of continuous research and development involving five hundred circuits had elapsed since the inventor received his first letter from Heavens.

———

During the time he was working on his project, Stocker also had negotiated for rights to utilize the Fallou circuit, the only essential feature of the new product that was not his own creation. Purchase of the U. S. Fallou patent from General Electric of France became final in August 1935. Thoroughly convinced by then of the ringing machine's potential, Fred Heavens enthusiastically agreed to join the inventor in forming a manufacturing company. Division of responsibility seemed quite clear. Stocker was to provide the engineering expertise, Heavens the initial financing.

A trade name for the new product came immediately. Stocker already had concluded that Sub-Cycle would be catchy and descriptive enough to be remembered by customers in telephone exchanges and manufacturing plants, their primary marketing targets. Heavens agreed.

Selecting a location for the company understandably was more complex. New York and Chicago were eliminated as being too large and still centers of Depression turmoil. Moreover, Heavens preferred to remain in his position at Telkor until the new company proved its success in the marketplace, even though the two organizations would be competitors. Based primarily on that priority, but with other considerations as well, the two men examined possible sites that would meet requirements.

Afterward, Stocker laughed heartily at the manner in which they made their "market survey." They wanted to be in a center of transportation but not in a large city, an industrial environment that wasn't dominated by unions, an area offering pleasant family living conditions, and, of course, something not too far from Elyria. "So with those things in mind," he said, "we simply looked at a map and selected Lorain."

———

C. PAUL STOCKER

Located on the shore of Lake Erie, twenty-eight miles west of Cleveland, Lorain, Ohio had observed its hundredth anniversary with a series of celebrations in 1934. Long before it was chartered in 1834, however, the village, then known as Black River, had prospered, first as a trading-post settlement, later as a hub for shipbuilding, fishing, and farming. Reincorporated in 1836 under the name Charleston, the village lost the momentum of earlier years and avoided the threat of becoming a ghost town only when a group of businessmen decided to build a railroad connecting the coal fields of southern Ohio to a lake terminal. That line, opened in 1872, awakened the town and led to an eventual railway network encompassing sections of the Baltimore & Ohio and Nickel Plate systems. Accessible by land and water, the village, renamed Lorain in 1874, was positioned for growth as an industrial center, despite being overshadowed by Cleveland.

A brass factory that became the city's largest employer in the mid-1800s, brought an influx of workers from New England, nearly doubling the population and prompting real estate speculators to buy up large areas of land throughout the county, also named Lorain. The opening of a steel company in 1894 attracted others from many parts of the country who had lost jobs in the serious depression of that decade. When Lorain experienced a labor shortage at the beginning of the twentieth century, a concerted effort was made to attract more workers from Germany, Scotland, Ireland, Italy, and Spain. Immigrants from Poland, Hungary, Yugoslavia, and Greece followed in the years preceding World War I. Consequently, the city became known as a melting pot community, represented by more than fifty nationalities. An interesting diversity of churches identified neighborhoods where international groups banded together to preserve their individual cultures.

In the throes of the Great Depression, Lorain suffered massive layoffs along with other areas of the country. Nevertheless, in 1935 the National Tube Division of U. S. Steel, the city's leading industry, produced more than 1,500,000 tons of ingots. American Shipbuilding Company continued to build the majority of leviathan ore carriers on the Great Lakes. Thew Shovel Company and American Stove Company were known around the world. American Crucible Products Company manufactured traffic signals and was recognized as a pioneer in developing high-leaded bronze bearings, nuts, rings, and pump liners. The B&O Railroad was making plans to build a three-million-dollar coal dock at Lorain, where the Black River emptied into Lake Erie.

A feeling of public optimism was starting to be reflected in the pages of the *Lorain Journal,* which recently had become the city's sole newspaper by purchasing its only rival, the *Times-Herald.*

Scores of smaller manufacturing companies also added significantly to the economy, but none had adopted the name of the city and county. Considering that a good omen, Paul Stocker and Fred Heavens agreed that the name of their new firm would be Lorain Products Corporation.

———

In September 1935, at a time when risk seemed synonymous with disaster, Stocker went to Lorain in search of both living and company quarters. The risk was intensified when Fred Heavens admitted that his commitment to "provide the financing" did not refer to a source of money, but rather to a knack for obtaining loans. This revelation was a severe and unexpected setback for the Stockers, but their exposure to adversity had given them an immunity against misfortune.

Articles of incorporation were duly filed on October 10, 1935 for "the manufacture, sale, and dealing in all kinds of electro-mechanical devices, and doing all things incidental thereto." Total capital of Lorain Products Corporation, half of which was contributed by each man, was five hundred dollars. Soon thereafter, Stocker transferred to the company exclusive rights to his U. S. patent for production of an electrical frequency reducing device that would become known throughout the telephone industry as the Sub-Cycle.

Beth Stocker resigned from her position in New York that November, after training another bacteriologist to take over her job, and joined her husband in Lorain, where they rented half of a duplex and began what she always would remember as the most trying year of their lives:

> The previous two years in the East had been difficult, but we were young and we didn't really feel that we were suffering so much. None of our friends there had any money either, so we all ate a lot of hamburger and got along fairly well. When we moved to Lorain, however, we realized we were taking a big chance by plunging in deeply, knowing we had to make it. I think the fact that our parents were rugged individuals had something to do with our determination to remain on our own.

Mrs. Stocker could not recall a time when her husband succumbed to discouragement. "If he had any doubt about eventually being successful, I never knew it," she said. "He always spoke in optimistic tones."

While making further plans and preparing manufacturing facilities during the last two months of the year, Stocker visited Western Electric Company in New York, explaining the advantages of his revolutionary Sub-Cycle. The reception was so favorable that he returned to Lorain with a written promise comparable to a purchase order, pending start-up of the new company.

True to his word, Fred Heavens proved that he did, indeed, possess an ability to skirt the need for advance funding. Having been a salesman for International Telephone & Telegraph Company, as well as head of Telkron during a business career of nearly forty years, his lack of money was offset by a wealth of experience and contacts. Armed with Stocker's drawings and the promissory letter from Western Electric, the two men obtained credit for all the materials, parts, and supplies they needed, including stationery. They convinced Acme Electric Company that an order for one hundred transformers would lead to many more in the future, if only they could receive the first delivery within thirty days and obtain an extension of ninety days for payment. Using the same technique, they ordered capacitors from Sprague Electric, relays from North Electric, and cabinets (encasements for the Sub-Cycles) from Riester & Thesmacher, a manufacturer of sheetmetal products.

In making these arrangements, Heavens advised his much younger colleague that payments should be made ahead of the ninety-day limits. He explained that such a policy would establish a reputation assuring them of easily obtainable credit in the future.

Immediate advertising in trade journals, was essential but unaffordable. As a solution, Heavens offered Suttle Electric Company, a Lawrence, Illinois jobber, one year's guaranteed distributorship of the Sub-Cycle in return for advertising it in *Telephony* magazine. The proposal was accepted and Lorain Products received its initial advertising for "The Greatest Engineering Advance in Ringing Machines since the Invention of the Telephone" sans cost, before financing more by using life insurance policies of the owners as collateral for bank loans. For many years, the preponderance of sales could be attributed directly to promotion through trade magazines.

On January 1, 1936 Lorain Products announced the official opening of its business. Office and manufacturing areas were combined in a rented upstairs back room at 671 Broadway in Lorain, next to a dentist's office.

"The room measured fifteen by twenty-one feet and contained everything our young company owned, much of which hadn't been paid for," Stocker said. A more detailed inventory revealed a typewriter and card table provided by Heavens and books, tools, and machinery owned by Stocker. Roland L. Smith, an accountant who actually had been hired before the opening to assist part-time in the bookkeeping, was the only employee (he did not obtain full-time status until the beginning of 1938). Beth Stocker and Emma Heavens served with their husbands on the board of directors.

At their first board meeting the next afternoon, the four directors elected Fred J. Heavens president and treasurer, C. Paul Stocker vice president and secretary. In addition, Heavens was named sales manager and Stocker chief engineer, with salaries established on an equal basis. Similarly, each of the couples received 125 shares of stock, valued at two dollars per share. The directors then adopted a resolution destined to have a profound influence on the company's evolvement:

> The stock represented by this certificate may not be sold, assigned or disposed of, in whole or in part, to any person except the members of the holder's immediate family, unless the holder of this certificate shall in writing first offer the same to the other stockholders of this company, any one or more of whom shall have the right to acquire the shares proposed to be sold, at the offered price, said offer to be accepted within ten days from the date of said offer. Said writing or option shall apply only to the entire amount of stock proposed to be sold, and shall not give unto any stockholder or stockholders any right to so purchase a part only of the shares offered.

With material now arriving from suppliers, Stocker began assembling the Sub-Cycles. Although Western Electric carried through with its purchase order for one hundred units, the first recorded shipment of the company's product was made to the Ironton-Arcadia Telephone Company on January 8, 1936. A letter from the Ironton, Missouri, company requested shipment "as soon as possible," because one of two batteries for its current ringing system was "nearly spent." The letter was among several already being received in response to the *Telephony* advertisement, which offered the machine for sale on a thirty-day trial basis.

A reply from Heavens to the manager of Ironton-Arcadia reflected the company's early modus operandi:

> We thank you for your letter, which refers to the new Sub-Cycle Ringing Machine, and we are shipping one of these today via express. We are sure that you will be much pleased with its operation. Full instructions are enclosed with it. Just follow them and after it is installed you can forget about it.
>
> In a few days we will have the descriptive bulletin from the printer and will send one to you. However, the

instructions will give you all the information needed to get it into operation. There are no moving parts in the Sub-Cycle and therefore nothing to adjust. Changes in input frequency of the power supply do not affect its operation and the input voltage can also vary substantially. On full load (20 watts) the output voltage will not drop more than 8 volts.

If you have any difficulty of any kind, notify us immediately. Also, if it is not too much trouble, we would appreciate hearing from you as to how it is going after it has been operating about a week. As against a battery-operated pole-changer such as you have, you will make a nice saving in using Sub-Cycle.

Stocker personally assembled the first hundred Sub-Cycles, classified as Model S (Standard). Despite the product's acceptance, several doubters warned that demand would dwindle quickly because of saturation in such a restricted market. Not in the least discouraged by such comments, Stocker projected long life and steady growth for the Sub-Cycle. Moreover, he had no intention of remaining a one-product company for very long, and he visualized immense opportunities for new products in an industry with unbounded potential.

Even with the Depression slowdown, the United States had seventeen million telephones, or more than half of those in the world. The familiar "number, please?" was being repeated continuously by operators at thousands of switchboards in all forty-eight states. New transmitters regularly replaced older models in an evolution that surely would continue into unimaginable stages, as both the Bell System and independent telephone companies grew. Telephone development in small U. S. communities was gaining momentum to the extent that it already exceeded the urban development in all but seven foreign countries. Each telephone system represented a possible customer, and Stocker had what he reported as "the opinions of many authorities" that the Sub-Cycle "was in a class by itself and would become the standard for all ringing machines for many years to come."

Although they represented a contrast in personalities, the

owners of Lorain Products had few disrupting disagreements in the early years of their relationship. Each respected the expertise of the other. Admittedly ungrounded in business affairs at first, Stocker trusted the advice of his seasoned partner. Heavens, on the other hand, showed only the minimum interest in engineering required for handling sales and orders. Bills were paid as much as thirty days ahead of their due dates and within six months a top credit rating was established with suppliers.

Heavens, then fifty-four years old, was described by friends as being "a somewhat fidgety man who spoke quickly, smoked cigars incessantly, and frequented local pubs." Stocker, at thirty-two, was reserved, choosing to ponder his thoughts before speaking out. Seemingly unshaken by stress, he puffed only an occasional pipeful of tobacco, and drank alcoholic beverages only on rare occasions. Both men were considered thrifty.

A humorous incident related by one of the company's early employees portrays both the thrift and smoking habit of Fred Heavens:

> Mr. Heavens smoked each cigar down to a soggy stub, which he frequently left on our work bench when he left the room. Often he would forget it, so after waiting several hours for him to retrieve the thing, I would throw it out into the alley. By that time I would almost be ill. So one day, in an effort to break him of leaving his cigars in my area, I selected a particularly bad example from the alley and placed it where he could see it on his next trip. Unfortunately, he came down from upstairs *without* a cigar and, upon spotting the dead stub, exclaimed, "Ah, I must have forgotten this." With that he popped it into his mouth without flinching, and his habit did not change.

Richard Oldham, who had just graduated from Lorain High School, was hired in the spring of 1936 to assist Stocker with the assembly work and free him for more engineering research. At about the same time, Oldham's sister June became secretary to both Stocker and Heavens.

In addition to selling regularly to Western Electric, the company added other major clients who were to account for a large portion of their business through the years. Among them were Commonwealth Telephone, Automatic Electric, Graybar Electric, Kellogg, North Electric, and Stromberg-Carlson.

Business having increased well beyond the three Sub-Cycles per day the two company officers considered a minimum for remaining solvent, they soon expanded into two rooms at 671 Broadway. By the the end of the first year, they began to look for quarters that would accommodate still further growth.

FOUR

BUILDING A COMPANY

When President Franklin D. Roosevelt made his second-term inaugural address on January 20, 1937, he offered assurance that America was on a steady course of recovery from the Great Depression. The previous year had ended on an encouraging note and economists forecast continued healthy gains in 1937. The telephone industry provided one of several indicators substantiating that prediction. With a 6.25 percent annual growth rate the total number of telephone installations was expected to soon match the 1930 peak of 20,201,000. Long-distance business was breaking records. Syndicated companies formed in the 1920s, but allowed to deteriorate or go into bankruptcy during the Depression, were being reorganized and rehabilitated. An experimental coaxial cable between New York and Philadelphia proved that hundreds of simultaneous two-way telephone conversations could be handled over one line. Like other industries, telephone manufacturers were beginning to resume dividends, after a lapse of more than five years.

Confidence in revived prosperity encouraged President Roosevelt to propose modifications of government-financed projects and a corresponding growth in private investments to the extent that he was accused by some supporters of the New Deal as turning sharply to the right.

Just when the economic momentum seemed secure, however, the business cycle began to arc downward. By mid-year the United States was falling into a recession, labeled by many as a new depression. The New York *Times* index of business dropped from 110 to 85, canceling all gains made since 1935. Employment plunged again, taking retail sales with it. Steel operations and automobile production, accepted barometers of general economic conditions, fell rapidly. Fortunately, the recession, although acute, was brief. But it emphasized a need for caution as a replacement for euphoria in the months ahead.

Lorain Products fortunes were to follow a similar pattern, but for different reasons.

Enthusiasm for the Sub-Cycle brought a steady growth of business in the first half of 1937. Customers answering the company's periodic questionnaires reported it to be "relatively trouble-free" and "seldom requiring maintenance." Some wrote that they had been able to install their Sub-Cycles in attics or other remote places, without giving them further thought.

Anticipating a continuation of the upward trend in sales, Stocker launched a search for someone who could help with production when necessary, but more important, who could assist in further development of the product line, which he considered vital to the life of the company. His viewpoint differed in this respect from that of his partner, who preferred to concentrate efforts on selling a proven commodity. The opposing opinions, however, did not constitute a source of serious contention.

After considering several persons with varying experience, Stocker chose a young senior engineering major at Fenn College in Cleveland. Although his employment had been limited to working at Thompson Products while attending college, George Pohm had attributes Stocker considered essential to the new position. Highly recommended by Fenn faculty members, he had an inventive mind, a genial personality, and a drive for transforming creative ideas into practical products. He too had built crystal sets and one-tube radios as a youth, and his extensive reading reflected an unquenchable desire to learn as much as possible about everything that caught his interest, particularly if it was related to engineering.

Pohm joined Lorain Products Corporation in June, immediately after graduating from Fenn. Within a very short time, he substantiated the confidence that had been expressed by his employer. Working closely with Stocker, he helped develop a series of modifications on the Sub-Cycle, corresponding to widespread advancements made in the overall telephone industry.

Through the years, George Pohm would become a leader within his company and known throughout the world of telephony. A man of imposing size and strength, he felt uncomfortable wearing anything except bib overalls at work. A friend who was with him on an installation project at Hudson, Ohio, described the "power and personality" of Pohm:

> George carried most of the load as we lugged a piece of very heavy machinery to the top floor of a building. After looking around, he said, "I don't know what kind of voltage they have up here, and I don't feel like going all the way back downstairs to find out." So he wet a finger and stuck it into a socket. I said, "George, you're crazy." But he said, "No, if I get a little zap it's 110; if I get a good zap, it's 220." He could tell too.

With business accelerating, Stocker and Heavens agreed that the time had arrived to invest in a building that could be remodeled to fit their company's engineering, manufacturing, and office requirements. They chose a structure at 200 Seventh Street in downtown Lorain. The two-story frame building admittedly was in questionable condition, but it offered the needed space, and the $6,000 price could be financed with a ninety-day loan for the 17 percent down payment and a five-year mortgage on the remainder. After purchasing some used furniture and making needed repairs, the company moved into its first wholly owned quarters in the fall of 1937. Office and laboratories were located on the upper story, leaving an entire floor for assembling and shipping Sub-Cycles. A small addition on one roof, immediately labeled the cubbyhole, provided space for a drafting table and accountant's desk.

The pleasure of ownership and expansion was enhanced by a flow of new orders running counter to the nation's economic reversal, and plans for advanced models of the Sub-Cycle already were being developed. By the end of the year, Roland Smith, the accountant, was becoming almost equally adept at soldering wire terminals and the company was ready to advertise for a part-time draftsman.

In the background, however, unexpected trouble was simmering. Almost without warning, it emerged suddenly as a problem that threatened to destroy the young company.

Customers in coastal areas of the country complained that cadmium-plated relays, serving as starting switches on the Sub-Cycles, were beginning to stick in the "closed" position. Whenever a power failure or overload occurred, the relay would not release. Consequently, attempts to reenergize the machine were futile.

Working nearly around the clock in an attempt to unscramble the mystery, Stocker, often assisted by Pohm, could not pinpoint a reason for the problem, let alone find a solution. The bewilderment, in fact, became increasingly intense as complaints arrived in growing numbers and from a gradually widening area of the country. Relays that had operated faultlessly for nearly two years but were now suffering a common ailment, would respond to no engineering treatment. There was no alternative except to provide replacements. Meanwhile, Stocker would have to solve the problem if his company was to stay in business.

Determined not to sacrifice any degree of company integrity, the cofounders placed advertisements in telephone publications assuring customers that any Sub-Cycle with a frozen relay could be returned for immediate repair, while a new one was installed in its place. There would be no charge for this work, even if a machine no longer was covered by warranty, and Lorain Products would pay the round-trip cost of shipments.

For several weeks, shipments of new products were surpassed by the numbers of defective models being returned, and express charges alone exceeded income. Money had to be borrowed to keep the plant in operation. Survival became a matter of speculation for some, but Stocker himself retained his usual calm. Apprehensions that surely must have plagued him under such circumstances were not recognizable to others, even his wife. Coworkers insisted that his overriding concern was that customers who put their faith in the company never be disillusioned.

Evidence indicated to Stocker that salt in the air's moisture somehow had an adhesive effect on the relays. This would explain why the earliest failures had occurred near the coasts. Concluding that a chemical, rather than an engineering, examination was needed, he contacted a former Ohio University classmate, Clarence R. Cooper, who had become head of the chemistry department at nearby Fremont High School. The two men had lived at the same rooming house while attending college, and Stocker had great respect for the intellectual ability of his good friend, who immediately agreed to help.

When the analysis was complete, Cooper concluded that moisture and dust in the air had triggered eventual erosion of the cadmium facing on the Sub-Cycle relay and that salt air indeed had speeded up the process. The answer, he suggested, was to replace cadmium with chromium as a plating material. One reason the idea had not been immediately apparent was that cadmium then was considered to be the premier plating metal.

With its chrome-plated relay, the Sub-Cycle redeemed its reputation as a trouble-free ringing generator, but the costly process of making replacements continued well into the summer of 1938. All this was accomplished by a total roster of six men and one woman, the only new employee during the first eight months of the year being William A. Lester, who responded to the newspaper advertisement for a draftsman.

In retrospect, a positive impact of the frozen relay misfortune extended well beyond surviving a crisis. Customers across the country remembered the company's resolve to honor its commitments, regardless of the cost, thus establishing a reputation cherished by Paul Stocker for the rest of his life.

The most important way to keep that reputation, Stocker often said, was to carefully select employees at all levels. Any employee should be "trustworthy, honest, have sufficient technical knowledge for the job, and follow a planned program for self-improvement," he insisted. Furthermore, persons thus representing Lorain Products should display conduct outside the company "beyond reproach," and be able to "manage their financial affairs so as to live within their incomes." Those whom he considered destined for leadership also should have "imagination with patience and perseverence." With a twinkle that often softened the seriousness of his tone without diminishing its sincerity, he acknowledged the rarity of finding anyone with all such desirable characteristics, but contended that it was possible "to find individuals with most of them."

In selecting employees, Stocker relied more on instincts derived from personal discussions than on references, and his interviews became legendary. Putting prospective employees at ease with his informal style, he would draw out their feelings about work habits, families, continuing education, smoking, loyalty, recreation, church and civic activities, and whether they had such hobbies as crocheting, knitting, or working on automobiles. From their answers, he could determine if they had manual dexterity, determination, and the ability to get along with other poeple. Those who were accepted later marveled at his ability to remember everything they had said, and few of them left the company.

Even in 1938, when the name Lorain Products Corporation still was relatively obscure, several professional acquaintances were aware of Stocker's ambitions and the types of creative persons he sought for future leadership roles. Among them was George Woodling, who taught patent law at Fenn College. When one of his students, Martin Huge, was ready to receive an engineering degree, Woodling advised him to talk with Paul Stocker.

During the interview that followed, Stocker concluded his distinctive line of inquiry by presenting some specific technical problems. He didn't ask for answers, but only whether or not the young engineer thought he could solve them. When Huge showed the necessary confidence, Stocker told him there was no opening for another development engineer at that time, but suggested he check again in about six months.

Prompted by the scarcity of jobs that still existed in the summer of 1938, as well as a highly favorable impression of Lorain Products, Huge enrolled in graduate school at Ohio State University. While he was there, he worked out his solutions to the problems posed by Stocker. These he mailed, along with a letter explaining, "I don't know whether you are interested in my ability to solve the problems you described, but here is how I would handle them." The reply from Stocker stated that Huge's job with the company would begin in September.

Martin Huge considered his early days with the company a good measure of the man who hired him:

> I began in the shop, because Mr. Stocker said he wanted me to spend one month working on assembly. At the time, I wondered how long my shop work really would continue, but I never mentioned it. On the first day of the following month, I reported to the shop as usual. He came in and said, "I told you at the end of one month you would go upstairs into the engineering department." So I went to work that day with George Pohm.

With emphasis remaining on research and development, variations were added to the company's product lines, but the original Sub-Cycle was basic to all modifications. Although individual achievement was highly regarded, most new designs were the results of cooperative efforts, and the company owned all patents. Stocker repeatedly expressed his conviction that "a lot of good can be accomplished if no one is worrying about who gets the credit." Playing politics within a company was destructive, he said, because everyone benefited from teamwork.

The spirit of cooperation was felt in all areas of the company's business. Heavens resigned his position at Telkor to concentrate on the sales and office management of Lorain Products; yet, a large percentage of sales was generated by trips Stocker and Huge made to Bell Laboratories, where they received assignments to design products not available elsewhere. (The situation was somewhat ironic in that Lorain Products normally competed with Bell Labs, which designed products to be made by Western Electric, its affiliate under the AT&T umbrella.) All qualified members of the company made service calls, and no one hesitated to help out in the assembly room when needed.

Stocker, who maintained an up-to-date library of patents, technical works, and scientific papers in several languages, "read government patent reports like other people read newspapers," according to one colleague. His inventions multiplied despite a growing amount of time spent in managing both the laboratory and assembly operations. Understandably, his focus was on the telephone industry, but the lure of other possibilities was tempting when he sensed an unfulfilled need elsewhere.

One diversion took him into lighting. Fluorescent bulbs wore out quickly under normal conditions, because their lives depended on the number of times they were turned on and off. Recognizing this as a deficiency in their impulse starters, rather than the bulbs, Stocker made extensive studies (assisted by Huge and Pohm) to determine that some of the coating was pulled off the cold filament each time a light was turned on. Consequently, he designed a circuit for quickly preheating the filament by the use of a transformer. Tests proved that the new system extended bulb life an incredible thousandfold over those using conventional starters. One major obstacle stood in the way of marketing, however: the Lorain Products starter created a few watts of wasted power. This problem could be corrected by redesigning the bulbs, but Stocker was not prepared to challenge Westinghouse or General Electric in that arena. Instead, Lorain Products patented the design and sold it to GE, which developed it into the revolutionary "rapid start" lamp.

———

Like other inventors, Stocker continually looked for better ways to do things. But he also emphasized caution in attempts to beat the competition, warning, "It is more important to be the best than to be the first."

Other favorite mottoes included: "One thing at a time and that done well is a very good rule for all to tell," and "A man is just as big as the thing that makes him angry." The latter was engraved on a plaque displayed in his home.

One of the few things he considered "big" enough to stir his own anger was the betrayal of a trust, whether it concerned a major business negotiation or a small piece of equipment. He expected people to be honest to the extent that employees were free to borrow equipment from the plant for use at home, and the company never installed a time clock.

The experience Stocker remembered from Ohio University thoroughly convinced him that education represented the most auspicious avenue to personal fulfillment. Not presuming to equate specific educational levels with degrees of achievement, however, he hastened to explain that the reference was to reaching one's individual potential, whatever that might be. At least, he reasoned, everyone deserved an opportunity to try, and he offered both encouragement and assistance to the men and women of Lorain Products.

It was with this feeling that Stocker advised his young draftsman, William Lester, to work toward an electrical engineering degree by attending night school in Cleveland. With a company personnel list of only eight at the beginning of 1939, advancement into an engineering job obviously would position Lester well for the growth Stocker envisioned. Lester followed the suggestion, but soon decided he "lacked sufficient interest" to continue the effort. "As I became more and more disenchanted with electricity, I kept an eye open for something more in line with my interests in either automobiles or aviation," Lester said. When offered a job with an aircraft engine accessories company, he accepted, although he wrote of being "sorry to disappoint Mr. Stocker."

Stocker indeed was disappointed, but not discouraged. Hundreds of employees and young people not connected with the company would enjoy the benefits of his dedication to education in the years ahead, and very few persons in promising positions would leave Lorain Products for other employment. Consequently, the Lester incident, a minor occurrence in the company's history, was significant only as proving to be an exception to the norm.

An interesting epilogue to the story was that Lester's replacement as draftsman was a young native of Lorain named Walter Krok, who got the job as a direct result of pursuing education, and whose career would lead to an intriguing climax normally confined to the pages of fiction.

Having graduated from high school in 1932, Walter Krok wanted to work his way through school, but part-time jobs were not available. As an alternative, he found work as a lathe operator at sixteen cents an hour, supplemented that income somewhat by playing violin in a dance band, and enrolled in the mechanical engineering program of International Correspondence School, better known as ICS. Although few knew of his entrepreneurial instincts, he managed to purchase several houses at sheriff's sales by borrowing enough from a bank to make down payments of a hundred dollars on each. Rentals barely covered mortgage payments at first but picked up substantially as the Depression pressure eased.

After William Lester left Lorain Products in 1940, Paul Stocker contacted ICS for the name of an outstanding student, hopefully a resident of northeastern Ohio, who might be interested in drafting and design. The schools' placement director replied immediately that such a person worked in Elyria and had a "straight-A record" in his engineering courses.

"I came home one day and found that a Mr. Stocker of Lorain Products was interested in talking with me," Krok recalled. "That was what I had been looking forward to all those years I was taking courses."

During the interview, Stocker learned that Krok not only was interested in drafting and engineering, but was eager to help on other jobs as well. That was of special importance because "drafting" in June 1940 still could include occasional stints at winding coils, making wire forms, preparing engineering samples, and assembling Sub-Cycles. Within a few days, Krok was headquartered in the rooftop cubbyhole, but spending an equal amount of time working with Pohm, Huge, Oldham, and Stocker. "We all worked together," he said. "If George needed help winding the coil on something he was developing, I did it. If there was a package that needed special lettering, I did it. It was a pleasure to be working with people who became your good friends."

When France fell to German troops and British forces were driven back across the English Channel in the summer of 1940, America's military-oriented production became recognized as a defense effort. "Great strength of arms is the practical way of fulfilling our hopes for peace and for staying out of this war," said a campaigning FDR. His future opponent, Wendell L. Willkie, agreed. Congress authorized defense expenditures of $12 billion, which in nine months was tripled to a figure exceeding the entire cost of World War I. By then, a Lend-Lease Act approved by President Roosevelt and passed by Congress also offered arms exports to nations whose defense was vital to that of the United States. Mobilization of resources was slowed by a need to retrain workers long idled by the Depression and confusion among an array of government agencies struggling to comply with the War Department's industrial plan. Nevertheless, economic revival, which had stalled again in 1939, was reflected in production of both military and civilian consumer products.

Objections to direct U. S. involvement in the war persisted, but preparations for increased business were being made by companies of all sizes.

Four additional Lorain Products employees hired in the first two years of the new decade enabled the company to organize what was referred to with an admitted touch of hyperbole as an "assembly line" for production of Sub-Cycles. With business returned to its upward trend, the owners increased salaries, issued Christmas bonuses, and instituted a Participating Salary and Wage Compensation Plan, which enabled employees to share in net corporate earnings. A formula weighing all aspects of wage and salary scales with years of service guaranteed impartiality.

With the telephone industry geared to the accelerating wartime economy, Lorain Products looked for more expansive quarters to replace the building it had owned for just four years. After considering several possibilities, the owners chose an abandoned building and property known as "Nos. 1102-1122 F Street" on Lorain's northeast side. At the same time, they began a search for someone to purchase the structure they occupied downtown.

The F Street property's dominant building was a one-story brick structure that had in turn been a toy manufacturing plant, a shop for rebuilding automobile engines, and a warehouse for the storage of beverages. Thick walls filled with sawdust enclosing what had been a cooling room remained as reminders of the warehousing era. A long, narrow frame building with tin siding occupied the back section of the property, its appearance and location suggesting that it was built originally as a barn. Two deteriorating double garages completed the layout.

Stocker's plan was to remodel the brick structure, providing approximately 10,000 square feet of floor space for all company functions. The "out buildings" would be left standing for possible storage purposes.

Arrangements for purchase of the new buildings were completed less than a week before the December 7, 1941 Japanese attack on Pearl Harbor (which triggered record peaks of telephone traffic in all major cities in the United States). Business continued at the Seventh Street building, however, throughout the first year of America's participation in World War II, while major renovation of the company's future quarters was underway.

Establishing a pattern that became a harbinger of future expansions, Stocker assigned some of the company's own men to the renovation project. Alvin A. "Al" Pfaff, who worked for a division of the Lorain Telephone Company before joining Lorain Products as its twelfth employee in 1942, remembered being on one of the crews:

Three of us who were relatively new to the company were working with George Pohm to get the new building ready for occupancy in December. We hired a couple of carpenters to shore up the building itself, but we were doing most of the other work. One day while Bill Chapin and I were hanging conduit, the city electrician came in and confronted us. He thought we were electricians from Cleveland who had come to Lorain without a permit. After ordering us to stop work, he asked where he could find our boss, so we pointed toward George Pohm, who was showing another of our men, Louis Paul, how to reline the boilers with bricks.

Stomping back to that area of the room, the city electrician ask George if he was in charge of this crew. "No," George said, "I just hand bricks to this fellow inside." When the city electrician insisted on finding the boss, George said he could be found at 200 Seventh Street. As soon as the man left, George called Mr. Stocker who, of course, was left with the job of providing the explanation.

Many years later when that same city electrician was given the responsibility of supervising installation of a new traffic-light system containing complex relays and such, he came many times to ask George for help in working out the circuits, and they became the best of friends.

After a great deal of effort and two mortgage extensions, Stocker and Heavens sold their Seventh Street property on October 11, 1943. Lorain Products by that time had been in production at F Street for nearly a year.

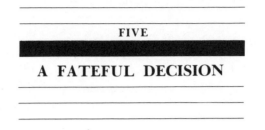

FIVE

A FATEFUL DECISION

Despite the growing emphasis on military manufacturing and the shortages of materials it created, production of consumer goods in 1941 showed a 25 percent increase over the two years since the beginning of World War II. Automobiles and furniture, along with various other household goods, were among the leaders. Arms exports and other aids to Great Britain were considered essential, but a strong public desire for neutrality combined with the long struggle to recover from the Great Depression elicited objections to increasing involvement in what still was considered by many to be a European war.

The attack on Pearl Harbor, however, quickly erased such objections, prompting an urgent mobilization unmatched in the world's history. Under the direction of a War Production Board, created on January 13, 1942, industries accelerated the conversion from consumer products to military manufacturing, using overtime and swing shifts to meet output demands. At the same time, a War Manpower Commission hurried to establish a balance between men who could enter the Armed Forces and those who should be frozen in essential jobs. Women filled resulting gaps in factory jobs previously limited to men. An Office of Price Administration was given the power to combat inflation through price and rent controls. New plants and airfields altered landscapes in many parts of the country, and population shifts to "war boomtowns" crowded some communities, depleting others. Railroads ran at full capacity without the need for a repeat of World War I government takeovers. The brief post-Depression interlude was ended. America was at war.

Like millions of others, Paul and Beth Stocker faced dramatic changes in both family life and business. During the previous five years they had purchased a home on King Street and started a family with the births of two daughters, Nancy in 1937 and Jane in 1940. The company had become integrated into the mainstream of the telephone industry, albeit at a rudimentary level, and life in a medium-sized city was progressing as they had hoped. They had even purchased a deteriorated weekend getaway cabin, which they were restoring on the shore of Old Woman's Creek, a well-known Lake Erie tributary in an area known as The Wetlands.

Now, however, thoughts were directed toward the nation's total commitment and the possible danger to one's family. Many years later, when World War II ended without the bombing of American cities, the latter concern was remembered almost as a fantasy. But at the time it was quite real. Lorain was located in the industrial belt stretching south and east from Detroit along Lake Erie, an area classified as a primary target for enemy bombers. Families and companies hung blackout curtains. Women took courses in home nursing. Men helped build bomb shelters, which contained emergency kits of food and medical supplies, and all citizens, including children, were taught what to do in case of an air raid. Cities and towns conducted air raid drills and civilian groups maintained vigils around the clock.

During the war years, Paul Stocker was one of many people who rode bicycles to work. He and Beth saved their allotments of rationed gasoline for visits to their parents. Rationing of other commodities, from tires to sugar and meat, became an accepted way of life, and Beth, along with most other women, canned a wide variety of food. Amid the changes, however, one pattern remained intact. In 1942, a third daughter, Mary Ann, was born to the Stockers.

When Dick Oldham left to join the Merchant Marine

Corps, Lorain Products lost nearly ten percent of its work force. The others soon were immersed in war-related production. Despite restrictions on expanding telephone switchboards to accommodate additional household subscribers, the tremendous need for business, government, and military communication throughout the country, as well as in war zones, prompted the company to continue designing new generations of Sub-Cycles. The most direct application to the fighting forces was a military version of the ringing generator for the Signal Corps, sold through Bell System channels. Because it would be required to work effectively in extreme ranges of humidity, George Pohm devised a method of packaging all components of the Sub-Cycle in an asphalt compound. Stocker was glad he had not torn down the two garages on the company's new property. One was used to house a tank where the compound was heated and poured around each unit, and the other became a "potting area" for final processing in preparation for shipment.

Similar units, also packed in the compound, later were sold to the Russian government. After the war, the same packaging idea was used briefly for the Sub-Cycle and subsequent products, but abandoned when it proved to be impractical for civilian use.

At the request of the U. S. government's Manhattan Engineering District, the company also designed and produced a special voltage regulator for top-secret research being carried out at the University of Chicago. Even the Lorain Products engineers who created the regulator were unaware that the experiments for which it was intended were being conducted by some three hundred leading scientists whose successful nuclear chain reaction would lead to development of the atomic bomb.

Throughout the war, Stocker hired handicapped persons to fill new assembly positions, beginning a practice he would continue after the formal Japanese surrender aboard the U.S.S. Missouri on August 27, 1945.

Reconversion following the war gave industrialists opportunities to expand technical concepts that had been nearly dormant during the Depression, then narrowly focused on military objectives. This knowledge at last could be directed toward strong sellers' markets created by shortages in housing, transportation, appliances, radios, and telephones, as well as experiments in such promising newcomers as television and automatic calculators.

As America thus began to revive a peacetime economy, it became clear to Paul Stocker that the Sub-Cycle alone could not continue to sustain adequate business growth. In considering other needs for improvements in telephony, he concluded that battery chargers used in telephone exchanges could be made more efficient and reliable through a concentrated engineering research effort.

At that time wet-cell batteries, about the size of an office desk, provided the direct current needed for telephone operation. Each time a receiver was picked up to answer a call, a small amount of power was discharged by the telephone exchange battery, which in turn was recharged by alternating current through a standard outlet. During a power failure, which could last for hours or days under adverse conditions, however, telephones had to work off the reserve in the battery. What was needed, Stocker reasoned, was a charger that could keep exchange batteries at full capacity, even during the demands of peak hours and power outages. Developing such a project seemed particularly logical for Lorain Products, since its Sub-Cycle provided power to ring the telephones. When the receiver was raised and a connection made, power was transferred to the telephone exchange battery.

Through the engineering efforts of Stocker, George Pohm, and Martin Huge, a special circuitry was created, and by the summer of 1946 a new type of battery charger was ready for the market. The first models worked well, except that a major component—the rectifier, purchased from outside suppliers—did not hold capacity well enough to meet the standards Stocker hoped to achieve. If the new battery charger was to become the revolutionary product its developers anticipated, Lorain Products would have to invent its own superior rectifier.

Although company engineers still worked together on research projects, Stocker liked to have one person assume primary responsibility for each. George Pohm and Martin Huge, who had developed a progressive series of products for the Signal Corps, had become engrossed in new models for civilian use, along with working on the battery charger. Rather than distract them from those assignments, Stocker approached chief draftsman Walter Krok with a surprising question: "How would you like to do something different by working on a rectifier?"

Krok, trained in mechanical, rather than electrical engineering, asked "What's a rectifier?"

Unruffled, Stocker patiently explained that the rectifier changed AC current to DC inside a battery charger, that he wanted to invent a new type using nonmetalic selenium, and that he would provide Krok with "some reading material" to study in preparation for working on the project.

"That isn't my line of work, and I didn't even take chemistry in high school," Krok said, "but if you trust me to take on such a job, I'll certainly be glad to do it."

Assuring the draftsman that he did have such faith in his ability, Stocker put together material by the end of the work day.

"I thought it would be a book or two, but at quitting time, he handed me a huge pile of materials," Krok said. "But I took it home and began what became many weeks of lengthy reading. In addition to that, I had to spend time at the library reading books on chemistry and physics, just so I could understand the things Mr. Stocker kept giving me. After about four months of this, he tested me by asking a lot of questions. I must have answered them well enough, because he said it was time to begin the experiments. I could tell that he already had ideas on what we would be doing, but he always asked for my suggestions too."

Building a partition around a sink in the drafting room, the two men stocked a makeshift laboratory with what Krok described as "a bench, a bunsen burner, and some crucibles and retorts." Then they acquired some selenium from Canada and launched the project.

"At one point," Krok recalled, "we set up a small stove-top oven, which Mr. Stocker heated with a blow torch to get the selenium up to temperature for an experiment. When it was about where we wanted it, the hinges melted and the oven fell apart. We stood there and laughed for a while, then Mr. Stocker went to his office and ordered a regular electrically operated lab oven."

Krok, remembering the experience as "part of the fun days," laughed again whenever he relived the incident. "I was watching the thermometer, and had just said we needed only two more degrees when the whole thing fell apart," he said.

Although Stocker was largely responsible for developing the selenium rectifier, Krok's assistance, as well as input from Pohm and Huge, was important. Stocker referred to the successful project as an example of working together without worrying about distribution of credit. In addition, while experimentation was being carried out on the rectifier, Pohm made a breakthrough in construction of a transformer (also a vital part of the battery charger) that provided a more constant voltage than had been achieved previously.

Because the new charging equipment could supply most of the load at a telephone exchange, the stationary batteries had very little current passing through them. Most important, in this type of "float charging" the voltage had to be high enough to keep batteries fully charged, yet not high enough to cause deterioration. Like the Sub-Cycle, the new product had no moving parts.

Named the Flotrol because of its float control, the new battery charger, with its selenium rectification and ferroresonant power transformer, was introduced into the telephone industry in early 1947. Acceptance was almost immediate. Within a short time it offered the assurance that Lorain Products was ready for further expansion.

Fred Heavens, having reached age sixty-five, was even less

inclined than before to put substantial capital into such a move. Stocker, still in his early forties, was equally determined that the time had arrived for a major thrust in both engineering and production. Faced with such a philosophical stalemate, the two founders seemed destined to dissolve their twelve-year relationship.

Under terms of their 1935 resolution, Stocker offered to purchase the half interest of his colleague, who preferred retiring to beginning a program of expansion, but it was difficult to establish an equitable price. After pondering that problem, the two men found a solution in the form of an appraisal by a large customer firm that wanted to buy Lorain Products. The price offered by that company was agreed upon as a reasonable guideline, but a serious obstruction appeared quickly and unexpectedly. Heavens insisted that Stocker pay him in cash within a very short time. If this condition could not be met, he would opt for an outside sale.

The situation justifiably could have seemed insurmountable to a relatively young family man with most assets already represented by his own half interest in the business. But impediments were not foreign to Stocker. Problems were to be solved, not worried about, and he remained confident that he could fulfill the prophecy of a mysterious Manhattan fortune teller.

During the ensuing few days, a swirl of activity produced a maximum bank loan and a roundup of personal financial resources, all of which still fell short of the needed cash. With the deadline closing in, Stocker contacted business acquaintances and friends. In response, ten men willingly purchased Lorain Products certificates representing little more than faith in the ingenuity of a man and the potential of his company. Among these bankers were old friends from Bell Laboratories and more recent colleagues, including Martin Huge, George Pohm, Roland Smith, Al Pfaff, and Walter Krok (Krok's ability to make a substantial investment was somewhat surprising because he never had mentioned buying and renting houses during the Depression, then selling them when the economy recovered).

The ordeal was magnified for the Stockers because Beth's father had recently died and her invalid mother was staying with them. Moreover, they had purchased a new home on Lorain's Lake Erie shore, fulfilling a long-time ambition.

When Stocker presented Heavens the required cash within the designated time limit, the older man admittedly was astonished. On April 17 he relinquished all interests in the company and officially resigned as director, president, treasurer, sales manager, and purchasing agent. His wife also resigned her directorship. As the new president, Stocker immediately named Martin Huge vice president and Roland Smith secretary-treasurer. Both men later became directors, filling the vacancies of Mr. and Mrs. Heavens. Beth Stocker remained the fourth member of the board. Upon retirement, Fred and Emma Heavens moved to St. Petersburg, Florida, where he died in 1971 at the age of 89.

Research on the Sub-Cycle and the Flotrol produced complementary benefits as new models appeared at an increasing rate. Specialized Sub-Cycles had such designations as Model B for the Bell System, Model C for the Ohio Pipeline Company (later replaced by Model CC), and Models M, M-1, M-2, and M-3. All used relays to initiate the starting transient and became known as "Relay Start" Sub-Cycles. After intensive experimentation, Huge developed a biased-core frequency divider, using a rectifier to eliminate the need for relays and to provide self-starting for the Sub-Cycle. The new model was acclaimed throughout the industry as an outstanding advancement in harmonic ringing machines, and despite many more innovations the company vice president developed during the course of his career, he always considered it the most important of his thirty-five patents. In 1949 another model, the H-M, extended the machine's operation to all five frequencies in the harmonic series—$16\frac{2}{3}$, 25, $33\frac{1}{3}$, 50, and $66\frac{2}{3}$ cycles. The following year, a three-phase Flotrol using magnetic amplifier circuits for output voltage regulation moved telephone exchange battery recharging into a new generation.

As Lorain Products prepared for the 1950s the pace of

research and development led one customer to observe that it was "the only manufacturing company I've ever known that has more people working in engineering than in production." Although it was an obvious exaggeration, the statement was an apt description of Paul Stocker's intentions as majority owner of the reorganized corporation.

Equally reflective of the new impetus was the hiring of H. T. McCaig as the company's first full-time salesman. A stately gentleman who was certified to preach in the Mormon Church, McCaig had been the Chicago area manager of Stromberg Carlson. It was claimed by some that he "knew the name of every owner of every telephone company from Chicago to the Pacific Ocean." Armed with a replica of the new battery charger, contained in a special carrying case, McCaig and his wife began a cross-country trek, demonstrating the Flotrol wherever he had a business contact. In his wake, the sales began to flow, and the staff began to grow accordingly.

Walter Krok was put in charge of selenium rectifier manufacturing operations. Paul Penfield, who had spent eighteen years in other areas of the telephone industry before joining Lorain Products in 1947, became the first head of a separate production department for the manufacture of Flotrol battery chargers.

It was decided that the long, narrow barnlike structure behind the main building on F Street should be replaced by a more substantial building that could become the Flotrol manufacturing center, with the front reserved for assembly of Sub-Cycles. There was, however, one slight vexation. A postwar city regulation in Lorain prohibited the company from getting a building permit for new construction. Al Pfaff, who by then had been promoted to production manager, told how the problem was overcome:

> We were able to get a permit for repairs, so we "repaired" the roof by putting on all-new sections. Then, during the winter of 1947, we repaired the inside walls, perfectly legitimately, by covering them completely with brick siding. So one evening in the spring

of 1948, some of us went out with a carpenter and cut
down the tin siding, making certain the new roof came
to rest on the inside brick walls. When employees came
in the next morning they found a solid brick building,
all done with two building repair permits.

When additional floor space was needed that same year for
manufacturing rectifiers, a second story was added to one
wing of the main building. Construction was carried out by a
Lorain contractor, T. J. Hume, beginning a long association
that placed more emphasis on mutual trust than detailed
contracts.

After losses in 1945 and 1946, Stocker was able to report a
doubling of sales and a healthy profit in 1947, along with a
rapidly widening base of products. Although employment
totaled only twenty-seven when Richard H. McMillan was
hired the following year as the first full-time coil winder for
transformers, Stocker said, "Some day there will be more
than a thousand people working here." If that should come
true, joining the company in 1948 could be propitious.
McMillan, a recent high school graduate who intended to
work at Lorain Products for a few months before launching a
career in construction, sensed such opportunity and remained. A year and a half later, at age nineteen, he became
supervisor of the coil winding department. By then company
employment had more than doubled.

A similarity in qualifications among several key employees hired after World War II reflected a continuation of
Stocker's rather unique method of selection. L. J. "Jim"
Goodell was invited for an interview when Stocker learned he
had made an automatic record player from an old clock
works, a small motor, and scrap machine parts, while attending Ohio Northern College. Goodell was given a job building models designed by George Pohm in the engineering
laboratory, and encouraged to use his ingenuity wherever he
saw an opportunity. Later, he too was to discover the value
Stocker placed on creativity.

Marion Pollard, forever nicknamed Snub after a character

in early Mack Sennett comedies, was hired to assist Martin Huge. When Stocker learned Pollard also was able to fix anything in the plant that needed repair, he asked, "Snub, how do you feel about becoming our maintenance man?"

"How do you feel about it?" Pollard replied in a whimsical tone that would become his trademark in the years ahead.

"I asked you first," said Stocker.

"Well, I would like it. I enjoy taking care of various things more than working in one area."

"You have the job," Stocker said, and Pollard began new duties that led to the title of maintenance superintendent, then formation of a separate department.

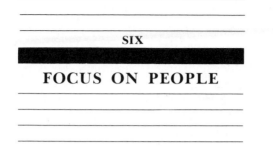

SIX

FOCUS ON PEOPLE

When Russia took control of Hungary after World War II, many Hungarian patriots who had worked in the underground opposition to Communist rule fled their country to avoid internment. Among them was Laszlo Laky, who escaped to Austria in the trunk of a friend's car. After obtaining a position as director of a refugee camp, Laky was joined by his wife, Zyta, and their three small children, who had walked over a hundred miles from Budapest to the Austrian border. Four years later, with no hope for a safe return to their country, the Lakys looked instead to the possibility of resuming a normal family life in the United States, where they had lived for a time while Laszlo obtained a master's degree from the YMCA College in Springfield, Massachusetts. To gain acceptance into this country, however, they needed proof of a guaranteed place to stay—something difficult to obtain in 1949 when Cold War tensions still clogged international immigration channels. In searching for a solution, Laszlo met a sympathetic American friend, Walter "Pat" Kilpatrick, who was working with the World Alliance of YMCAs at European refugee centers. Kilpatrick contacted his sister, Beth Stocker, and arrangements soon were complete for the Hungarian family's move to Lorain, Ohio. The plan called for them to live with the Stocker family for two or three months while they looked for a more permanent residence. By the time they arrived in the summer of 1949, Stocker had found Laky a job at American Stove Company in keeping with his business management expertise. The temporary stay at the Stocker residence extended to eight months, but Beth described it as an outstanding experience:

It was wonderful for our children, as well as theirs, because they matched all three ages. The Laky family slept in the attic, which we fixed up for them, and they lived in the basement most of the time. They did not want to share the entire house, although we insisted they use the living room and kitchen. The children didn't speak English when they arrived, but they learned it so quickly they soon moved into their proper school level and got top grades. We considered them almost part of the family, and they even went with us to our annual Thanksgiving gathering at Paul's boyhood farm.

Laky eventually was transferred by American Stove to Oklahoma, then California, where his wife, a talented artist, opened a successful studio. One of the two sons became an engineer, working at Lorain Products for a time before moving to Canada. The other became an architect in California, and the daughter applied her inherited artistic talent to textiles in her own West Coast business.

In a city known for its unusually high percentage of international representation, the Laky family experience paralleled an established Stocker reputation for hiring immigrants, as well as persons with handicaps. Examples reported in newspaper articles and by word of mouth quoted Stocker as praising these people for their "honesty, work ethics, and established self-discipline," explaining, "I'm happy to train employees for their jobs, but I hate to have to teach them how to work." Evidence left no doubt, however, that he was also motivated by strong humanitarianism.

As a Polish youth, Bruno Krol spent eighteen months with his family in Siberia after his father was arrested for fighting against Russia in an earlier war. Freed through the Polish Exile Treaty of World War II, he was drafted into the Polish Army, which was taken over by the British government. Trained in England, he fought in the Normandy Invasion as a tank operator, then lost a leg during a bombing raid in France. After recuperating in an English hospital, Krol remained in the British army until he was discharged in 1949. Two years later, under terms of a congressional act, he emigrated to Lorain, where he met Dick McMillan and was offered a chance to talk with Paul Stocker about obtaining employment. He always remembered that interview:

> Mr. Stocker asked me about my life, and seemed interested in knowing all the details. When I told him I had tried working in a British factory, but the loss of a leg made it impossible to meet the requirements, he said, "Never mind; we'll see what we can do for you." Then, after he checked a few things, he said, "You have a job for a lifetime." I couldn't use the winding machine to do my job, but he arranged for Snub Pollard to build a special one for me. He stopped many times after that to see if I was all right, and to ask more about countries where I had lived. Over a period of time I told him just about everything I remembered, but he had read so much he knew Russian and English history better than I did.

Later, Stocker was introduced to Irene Szabo at church. Although she spoke no English, having just arrived from Hungary, he learned through an interpreter that she had been forced to abandon a promising singing career when the Russians bombed Budapest, destroying her home and killing her two brothers. When the Hungarian Revolution began, she walked to Austria, then went to Germany, where she boarded a plane for the United States. A complete stranger in Lorain, unable to speak the country's language, and with no working experience other than singing, she desperately needed a job. Within two months she was at work in the Sub-Cycle Department of Lorain Products.

"Each morning during our break, a man came through the plant selling lox and cream puffs," she said. "I really eyed those cream puffs with great desire, but I needed every penny I could save to get started in this country. Somehow the word got to Mr. Stocker, and a cream puff began arriving at my desk every morning. Eventually, I asked an English-speaking friend to have him stop. I was putting on weight. As I began to learn English and he stopped to talk to us at our jobs, we both laughed about that." She retired twenty years later as a supervisor, with widespread local recognition for her singing.

Walking through the plant in the 1950s, as Stocker did each day, it was not unusual to find employees just learning to speak English. At times they were grouped with others of similar descent who had become bilingual. "In that way," said one, "we learned the language fairly fast, and had fun doing it."

Some women were hired when Stocker learned they had become widows without sufficient financial provisions for the future. One man got a much-needed job even though Stocker knew he had terminal cancer.

"He was the most compassionate person I ever knew," said Dick Pavelka, who joined the company in 1955 as an assembler, resigned to join another firm two years later, and was accepted back when that venture failed to meet his expectations. "He had been through hard times as a young man and suffered some early reverses in business, and I think he remembered them all so well he just didn't want to see anybody hurt. Somehow he was able to combine such warmhearted feelings with strong leadership." When Pavelka retired, he was product manager of ringing, tone, and signaling systems.

With the single exception of Richard and June Oldham, who were among the original three employees hired in 1936, the company had followed a policy of hiring only one person from a family. This seemed to be in keeping with a prevalent industrial philosophy of the times. After considering suggestions by several key employees at Lorain Products, Stocker became convinced the restriction no longer was warranted, and in the spring of 1952, he hired John Pfaff, brother of company veteran Al Pfaff, as an oven operator in the transformer area. From that point forward, employment of multiple family members became a valued tradition at Lorain Products. John "Porky" Pfaff, who eventually became a material planner, was one of several persons who followed other members of their families into responsible positions.

The president's office always was open to employees. Complaints could be aired there in guaranteed confidence unless they constituted direct accusations against another person. In such an instance, the president often would say, "Let's all talk about it," whereupon he would usher the accused person into the conference. "He was a great mediator because he understood individual personalities, and he knew how to handle people in all types of situations," recalled one employee who said he had learned that lesson first-hand in one of the office arbitrations.

Stocker could be stern when circumstances demanded it, but he preferred other means of maintaining authority. One favorite recollection of several employees was an incident when they were working at a pace that seemed unsatisfactory to the president. When he made that feeling known, one of the men said, "You know, Mr. Stocker, Rome wasn't built in a day." Without losing his serious expression, Stocker replied, "That's because I wasn't bossing the job."

Pace indeed was important to Stocker, but it was not simply equated with increased speed. "Mr. Stocker believed in getting jobs done as expeditiously as possible, but he didn't think employees should be pushed to extremes," Dick McMillan said. "I remember telling him once that I didn't think people in my area were working as hard as possible. Well, he became very thoughtful and answered, 'Dick, when you are out in the yard mowing the lawn and your neighbor is out mowing also, don't you occasionally stop at the fence and chat a little? And maybe your wife will bring you out some iced tea.' That is the way he understood people, and it worked. We all did our best because we didn't want to let him down, not because we felt a gun at our heads."

When employees became flustered, Stocker took them into his office, calmed them down, and again with an inventor's patience, talked about their problems, emphasizing that there always is a way to "think things through to a satisfactory conclusion."

At the same time, Stocker drew a distinct line between the need for constructive thought and wasting time, placing lengthy meetings in the forefront of the latter category. At a meeting, he would get out his watch, place it on the table, and say, "We have one hour to discuss this, and I expect that it will be brought to a conclusion at that time. If there is no conclusion, I will cast the deciding vote and we will proceed accordingly." To reinforce the pronouncement, he often substituted a small timer for the watch. At the end of the prescribed time, the buzzer would signal an abrupt end to the meeting.

"He felt so strongly about keeping time commitments that he once took his timer to church, warning the minister before hand that he was going to use it to check the twenty-minute sermon," daughter Nancy once said. "Well, the sermon was a little long, and Dad's timer went off on schedule. Mother was furious, although she maintained her composure, but the minister took it in stride."

There were many such examples of Stocker's business philosophy extending into his family life. Perhaps most memorable was his use of notes written on two-inch squares of blue paper. Different opinions existed on how the practice originated, but most agreed that the first batch was delivered by mistake from an order for large sheets of blue paper. Pinpointing the origin, however, was irrelevant in comparison with the proliferation of the small blue missives that appeared regularly at desks, work benches, and laboratory tables throughout the plant for the remainder of Stocker's career. Messages ranged from a simple "Call me" to a specific idea for improving a manufacturing procedure.

"It was amazing how much Mr. Stocker could write on one of those tiny pieces of paper," observed Jim Goodell, who kept some of them as souvenirs after he retired. "He believed that most written messages, like most meetings, were too long anyway, and he enjoyed making a point on a little blue note. Using tiny handwriting, he could put a world of information on one of those things, always making certain each was initialed and dated.

Similar memos at home were used to pass on ideas and telephone messages for the children. Each contained date, time, and initials. "Absolutely everything that came out of this household had to have that information on it," said daughter Jane.

Stocker's insistence on dating all communications, from sales brochures to two-word reminders, could be traced in part to the same trait in his mother. His wife, however, said a greater influence came from his work at Bell Laboratories, where dating all materials was essential for the protection of future patents.

Continued daily walks through the plant, where he still could address every employee by name, contributed to an accumulation of paper work that he dutifully handled on weekends when the company was closed. But like his father, he rarely missed having meals with his famly. At 12:05 P.M. each day he appeared for a half-hour lunch consisting of soup, a sandwich, a glass of water, and an apple. After his meal, he lay down on the living room rug, glanced at a clock on the mantel to decide how long he could rest, put a news-paper over his face, and went immediately to sleep. At the predetermined time, he arose completely refreshed, and returned to work, arriving by 1:00 P.M. "He had an internal clock that would awaken him in twelve or fourteen minutes, or whatever he decided," Nancy said. "He felt those naps were very important in helping maintain his energy, and he would rearrange office schedules that interfered with his coming home at noon. The only exceptions to the routine were Thursday noons, when he faithfully attended Lions Club meetings."

Dinner always was fun for the children because their parents would create games from interesting ideas. One favorite was a continuing exercise in judging lengths. Stocker would hold his hands apart and ask each daughter to guess the distance between them. Eventually their estimates (which he checked with a ruler) became amazingly accurate. Stocker considered it only a game, however, because in the plant he often cautioned employees, "Never guess when you can measure."

His celebrated composure at work was matched in many ways at home. Once when Beth was in the kitchen, the pressure cooker exploded, spreading prunes over floor, ceiling, and walls. Hearing the commotion, her husband rushed in, saw that she was all right, went for a stepladder, and said, quite calmly, "Well, let's start the cleaning."

During evenings at home, Stocker liked to sit in a favorite leather chair with wide arms to read business material he always brought from the office in a briefcase. Despite that concession to being a workaholic, however, he welcomed interruptions for reading to the children. "I remember sitting on the arm of that leather chair while he read *Grimm's Fairy Tales* and other books to us," Mary Ann said many years later. "Mother also read to us often, and that practice has passed down through our families."

Beth and Paul always were supportive of each other in disciplining their children, and both believed strongly that it was important not to display anger. "I'm sure they must have been angry at times, because that is human nature, but we never saw signs of it," said Nancy. "In fact, we also were expected to control anger. It was a taboo in our family."

All three daughters wore their long hair in braids, and as the eldest, Nancy wanted to have hers cut when she was in the fifth grade. Her father would not even consider such a possibility, however, and it was two years before he finally gave in to her pleas. "I don't know whether there was some negotiation between my parents, or he simply decided that I was old enough when it was time to enter junior high school," she recalled, "but I do remember it as a period when I had a difficult time conforming with the rule about controlling anger."

Stocker was described by all three girls as a strong disciplinarian, but never unreasonable. "We had an authoritarian family, but we were very close and happy, and we did things together," Nancy said. Mary Ann recalled also that, "Mother

talked much more than dad; he said she was the communica-
tor in the family. He was so punctual that he always seemed
to be waiting for mother—sometimes emphasizing that point
by sitting in the car with the motor running—but I don't
remember one instance when he complained openly about
it."

Lorain Products picnics at the property on Old Woman's
Creek were annual events, enjoyed by all members of the
company, even the year that a sudden downpour forced
everyone inside the cabin, where they discovered that the roof
leaked so badly everyone got wet anyway. As employment
outgrew the creekside facility, picnics were moved to the
Stocker home, then to other locations.

———

In the late 1940s demand for telephone service increased
nearly as much as in the twentieth century's first four decades
combined. Whereas companies previously kept engineering,
construction, and installation of facilities ahead of the
demand (so service would be available when customers
wanted it), they now were being forced to play catch-up. The
situation was attributed partly to the wartime moratorium
on private customer solicitations, but also to erroneous
prognostications. Many leaders in the telephone industry
had postponed immediate postwar expansion of existing
capacity in anticipation of a serious mid-century economic
depression that would leave new equipment unused. Instead,
technological innovations and the 1950 Communist invasion of South Korea combined to stimulate business and
industry.

Bell and its rival independent telephone systems began the
1950s in strong growth patterns aimed at recovering the lead
time they had fostered earlier. In some cities, the previous
underestimation of demand still created backlogs in delivery
of equipment, with exchanges operating at up to 98 percent
of capacity. Charles A. Pleasance, who contributed several
inventions as well as a published chronicle to the history of

independent telephones, used Lorain's twin city, Elyria, as an example of the sudden need for expansion:

New telephone numbers could not be assigned. If someone moved into an area within this exchange, he was given the same number that had been assigned to the former occupant. Telephone numbers became as permanent an accessory as a street address. The notion of receiving a private [one-party] line when the previous occupant had a five-party line could not be considered. But if the previous homeowner had been blessed with a one-party line, the number would probably be taken away and given to a business customer as soon as the telephone company was notified of the change. Many business customers were forced to continue with the five-party service they had subscribed to during lean times even though they could finally afford and needed one-party service.

Transistors were beginning to replace vacuum tubes in some communication devices, and long-distance dialing offered a welcome new convenience for telephone subscribers. Lorain Products, at the same time, introduced new three-phase Flotrol rectifiers employing magnetic amplifier circuits for output voltage regulation.

In 1951 the company added 14,000 square feet to the rectifier manufacturing and light assembly areas of the main building. Two years later, after Bell Laboratories issued specifications covering many more of the company's products, resulting in additional business from Western Electric, Stocker again hired T. J. Hume Company to construct a somewhat smaller brick addition for its first sheet metal fabrication shop. Employment at Lorain Products for the first time exceeded one hundred.

With the new addition nearly completed in July 1953, Paul Stocker took his family on its first trip to the western part of the country, believing it was important that they "know the beauties, vastness, and variety of our country." It was, in fact, the first time the Lorain Products president himself had been west of Chicago, and to assure full attention to the trip, he telephoned the office only once a week.

On July 22, two weeks before Stocker's intended return, welders were joining steel beams from the addition under construction to those of the structure erected in 1951 when sparks from an acetylene welding torch ignited tarpaper sheathing. (Ironically, the new structure was to replace small wooden outbuildings recently torn down because they were considered fire hazards).

After attempting unsuccessfully to stop the blaze with hand extinguishers, welders called the fire department, which arrived at 2:14 P.M. By then, flames were spreading through the building's roof loft, threatening to destroy the entire company complex. Two hours later, with an estimated 1,000 spectators looking on and one enterprising young vendor selling them popsicles and ice cream, the fire was quenched, but the rectifier unit and several offices were destroyed. Fire Chief Clarence Farschmann and a member of his crew were burned slightly in the $100,000 blaze.

Early the next morning Vice President Martin Huge received his regular weekly telephone call from Stocker, who was in Idaho. "We've had a terrible fire," Huge said, "and you had better get back as soon as possible."

After listening to complete details of the disaster, Stocker asked, "Is the fire completely out?"

"Of course," replied Huge.

"Have you contacted the insurance people?"

Again, Huge said, "Of course."

There was a moment of silence, then the soft voice of Stocker, "Okay, I'll see you in two weeks."

———

At its homecoming in October 1953, Ohio University made final plans for a sesquicentennial celebration during the coming year. Keystone of the observance was to be an Alumni Sesquicentennial Scholarship Fund drive. Dr. John C. Baker, president of the university since 1946, for whom a recently completed university center later would be named, declared that such building projects were "not as significant for the future of Ohio University as a sound scholarship plan that can grow from this sesquicentennial beginning." The president also announced a slate of new Alumni Association officers to serve during the sesquicentennial year. Among them was Vice President C. Paul Stocker, who also had agreed to head the fund drive in Lorain County. This dual assignment marked the first time Stocker became actively involved in affairs of his alma mater, although he had visited the campus often and had recruited Ohio University engineering graduates for employment at Lorain Products. With the beginning of 1954, he and his wife also became donors of a $2,500 scholarship to help launch the campaign. The following year, Stocker inaugurated and headed a drive among Ohio University engineering alumni to send Dr. D. B. Green, chairman of the Department of Electrical Engineering, to a meeting of the International Commission on Illumination in Zurich, Switzerland.

SEVEN

PROBLEMS AND
SOLUTIONS

Baffling problems infiltrating what appears to be a reliable manufacturing pattern can test the mettle of a man or a company. After the fire of 1953, Lorain Products was forced to purchase rectifiers from an outside source while its facilities were being restored. Even with the Flotrol now representing the company's largest source of income, however, the situation was considered little more than a temporary inconvenience. Research and designs for proposed advanced Flotrol models indeed continued during the six-month interruption before selenium rectifier production again went on line. But a new enigma was soon to emerge.

With no change in procedures, rectifiers that were manufactured in single discs, then assembled into groupings of various sizes, began to fail. Unable to identify the problem, Walter Krok, who was in charge of selenium production, called upon the combined expertise of Martin Huge, George Pohm, and finally Paul Stocker. Detailed analysis of the selenium and aluminum raw materials revealed nothing. Heating, bathing, and etching followed exact specifications. City utilities records indicated that nothing had been altered in the water works treatment process. Walter Krok worked nearly around the clock, catching occasional sleep on a cot in the plant, while the search for a solution went on and the company again resorted to outside purchase of rectifiers. After several weeks, with reasonable ideas seemingly exhausted, someone in the group suggested the remote possibility of tracing the problem to the soap product DUZ, used in a cleaning stage. Contacting Proctor & Gamble in Cincinnati, Stocker discovered that yes, a chemical change had been made in the DUZ formula, offering an improvement for household use. Would P&G produce a special batch of the old-style DUZ for investigative purposes? Of course. And the problem was solved. Something in the newer formula had seeped microscopically and disastrously into pores of the selenium, but none of the defective products had ever been shipped.

Back on track, the company in early 1954 made plans to erect a new building for expansion of selenium rectifier manufacturing. "The decision was not arrived at hastily," Stocker explained in a report to stockholders. "In view of the fact that germanium and silicone rectifiers were being developed at a rapid pace, consideration was given to the possibility that demand for selenium rectifiers would decrease. Because of improvement we made on selenium rectifiers in our own laboratories, however, we felt justified in going ahead with the new building."

Stocker's initial plan was to build directly west of the F Street plant by purchasing adjacent homes that could be razed. When it became evident these were not for sale, however, he reset his sights on fourteen parcels of primarily vacant land occupying five acres south of the Nickel Plate Railroad tracks bordering the plant. Although only two houses were located there, the area was zoned residential, so purchases were made first on options, taken up after the district was rezoned. With these delays, construction of the brick building known as Plant 2 was started in the fall and completed the next year. In addition to its manufacturing section, the single-story building housed laboratories, offices, loading facilities, and a heating plant.

Construction of Plant 2 on G Street was historically significant in several respects. It marked not only the first move across the railroad tracks into what would become the company's major factory area but also the beginning of a long-range plan to acquire homes that could be held and rented until razed to make way for further expansion. In addition, it led to growth of a sales force, and cemented Stocker's belief in having qualified company personnel work alongside the general contractor, T. J. Hume Company, in designing projects and overseeing construction.

After plans had been completed, footers laid, and forms begun for pouring concrete, Jim Goodell, "on loan" from laboratory and maintenance assignments to help install wiring for the new building, proposed what he considered a better placement of conduits. Stocker mulled over the suggestion, sketched a few drawings, and said to Goodell, "That's a very good idea, and, by the way, maybe you should begin to look after this to make sure everything goes together right for what we will need." By the time the project was completed, Goodell was plant engineer, a position he would hold for the next three decades.

"There was no official announcement or bulletin saying I was going to be plant engineer," Goodell said. "I just kind of evolved into the position."

Stocker admitted to a dislike for designating specific titles and listing duties at supervisory levels, and he hated organizational charts. Goodell, like many others, agreed with the president. "Mr. Stocker expected people to do certain things, but the more you did, the more responsibility you developed, and the more you got ahead," he said. "Job titles and lists seemed too confining for that philosophy."

In preparation for completion of the new factory, Stocker hired veteran telephone man J. E. Yarmack as sales manager of the Rectifier Division. A Russian refugee who had fled to the United States at an early age, Yarmack had earned electrical engineering degrees at M.I.T. and Yale. Since 1939, he had held sales positions with the Federal Telephone and Radio Corporation, International Rectifier, and Syntron. In preparation for his new position, Yarmack assisted H. T. McCaig, who continued as head of corporate-wide sales.

Net income for 1954 almost doubled that of the previous year, partially because of congressional removal of the excess profits tax on corporations, but attributable also to the increased sales effort. Stocker's instructions to keep inventories low were reversed when the first quarter of 1955 brought an unexpected further increase, reaching 170 percent of that recorded in the same period of the previous banner year. "Competition is keen, but we are holding our own," the president reported. "In fact, a mad scramble is going on to meet the increased demand." There remained no further question on the decision to construct Plant 2. Instead, the board of directors now considered the possibility of erecting a Plant 3.

Although the company manufactured many component parts of its major products, as well as its own machinery, some things still were purchased from outside sources. Primary among them were magnetic units. This dependence, Stocker pointed out, presented an "obstacle to increased production" and a threat to "improving the present record of delivery." With one of the company's departments already producing magnetic units in very limited quantities, Stocker saw the experience thus available as the basis for "a logical move toward expansion of this department through construction of another new building on G street." Consequently, company engineers prepared plans and specifications, which were approved by Stocker in late 1955. Again, the prognosis proved correct. Lorain Products received more new business in January 1956 than in any previous month in the corporation's history. By September, Plant 3, equipped with overhead cranes, three gas-fired ovens for baking transformers, a high-temperature furnace, custom-made winding and impregnating machinery, and test positions, was in full operation. (Just before the opening of Plant 3, Stocker was named a fellow of the American Institute of Electrical Engineers.)

Three months later, production again was setting new records, and employment had jumped to 227. Additional Flotrol models were being brought out regularly by research engineers, and a new teletypewriter power supply design had been submitted to Bell Laboratories for approval. Developed by Huge, the unit featured a self-saturated magnetic amplifier for voltage regulation. After it was later applied to a wide range of products, the amplifier became one of the company's largest dollar-volume items.

A popular carrier supply unit introduced in 1956 also captured the interest of the Bell System and was soon to go into production. At the same time, what Stocker referred to as "considerable missionary work" was being carried out with the associated Bell companies in an effort to interest them in further use of Flotrol battery chargers. "It is anticipated that this will move slowly," he reported to colleagues, "but once the ice is broken, we feel real progress will be made."

For the first time since the company's reincorporation nine year years earlier, one of the shareholders offered to sell his stock to the corporation. This necessitated setting a price on shares—something that had never been discussed. Because resale of such securities as soon as possible after their purchase by the corporation was considered desirable, directors voted to reduce the per-share value to a level enabling prospective buyers to invest either large or small amounts. Based on that premise, the board authorized the issuance of new shares in exchange for the old on the ratio of two hundred for one. The company's attorney subsequently was authorized to calculate an equitable price, which was kept confidential among shareholders.

At the end of its twentieth year, Lorain Products had reached the optimistic expansion mode that its cofounder and current president never had doubted. The main plant had been expanded three times since World War II, a second plant was producing selenium rectifiers, and less than a year later, a third and larger structure for production of magnetic units and transformers was completed. Others already were being forecast for the future as the company began 1957 by leasing a warehouse at Broadway and Tenth Street to store raw materials and an inventory of finished goods. A separate Design Department, headed by Paul G. Penfield, was organized, and the Production Department, under the supervision of Al Pfaff, was expanded. Advanced models of Flotrol battery chargers were being designed for old customers and for new applications. A transistor-powered Sub-Cycle for multifrequency ringing captured strong interest at a national convention of the Independent Telephone Association. The full lines of both Flotrol and Sub-Cycle machines received approval of the Canadian Standards Association, boosting what already showed promise of heavy sales in that country. Stocker felt "constant pressure to establish a Canadian subsidiary" because of duties and taxes that increased the cost of equipment to Canadian customers by 40 percent, but preferred to move slowly in that respect while stabilizing the effects of myriad transitions at the Lorain plants. Export sales to other nations around the world also showed steady growth, albeit small in comparison with the potential of domestic marketplaces.

To better penetrate U.S. markets now that manufacturing capabilities were increased substantially, the company felt an accompanying need to bolster its small sales force. Top executives, including President Stocker and Vice President Huge had continued to assume part of that responsibility even after hiring McCaig and Yarmack, but the rapid growth of the 1950s was shrinking the time they could devote to direct sales. The need was sharply magnified when Sales Manager McCaig died in September 1957. Yarmack then became head of all company sales, and Eldon Miller, formerly with the Kellogg Switchboard and Supply Company, was hired as sales engineer for the Midwest and Far West. As part of that move, Lorain Products Corporation in December established its first official Chicago-area office at 9500 West Ogden Avenue in suburban Brookfield, under Miller's direction, even though the company's presence there was limited at that time to desk space and an answering service.

To complete the nucleus of what would expand into a sales department, Stocker hired an experienced sales engineer, Charles "Chuck" Ramaley, a University of Pittsburgh electrical engineering graduate who had worked for the U. S. government and, more recently, with Syntron. Ramaley had sold rectifiers to Lorain Products when the 1953 fire curtailed the company's own production. Fred Davis, who had retired from the Automatic Electric Company after a long career in which he gained respect throughout the industry, was hired as a part-time sales representative for the eastern U. S.

(During the next ten years, the sales group would expand to a network of ten district offices and a home office staff of fifteen, headed by Ramaley after a heart attack prompted Yarmack to request a less pressurized position at the San Francisco office in 1961.)

All members of the sales staff were reminded by Stocker that good customer relations were vital to the company's health. There was no such thing as a "bottom line" in sales, he said. Instead, each was "a beginning toward further sales," and every customer was to be reminded of the company's reputation for standing behind its products.

To assure the continuation of this integrity through the complexities that came with growth, the president realized service "in the field" could no longer be provided adequately by taking engineers off regular jobs for spot assignments each time assistance was requested by a customer. Someone should devote all his energies to customer service. Stocker's choice, after conferring with Huge, was Frank Borer, a World War II Army Air Corps veteran who had joined the company in 1949 as a Flotrol assembler. At one time, when the company still was small, Borer built complete units starting with winding coils, making transformers, assembling and testing units, and visiting customers to make repairs. Meanwhile, at Stocker's suggestion, he had taken correspondence courses in electrical engineering.

In selecting Borer for the job, Stocker typically avoided formalities. Instead of announcing creation of a new position, he talked with Borer about field assignments, introduced him to personal friends in customer organizations, and let the job evolve from part-time to full-time status. Borer reflected:

> I can't even remember a specific date on which I actually became the service manager, but I certainly remember the indoctrination. Mr. Stocker supported anything that would give service to a customer. If you sold

- 83 -

something for $500 and it cost $1,000 to repair it, that's what you did. Making the customer happy not only was the decent thing to do, but also good business, because the next time that same customer wanted to buy a $5,000 product, he would be knocking on your door. And that was the basis of Mr. Stocker's philosophy. People talk about service all the time, but providing it to the extent of Mr. Stocker's commitment is extremely rare.

Borer's 1956 yellow Buick soon was recognized at customer locations and convention sites across the country as he fostered friendships, gave assurances of ongoing service, and took care of specific requests. Repair work always was provided without charge, regardless of the length of time a product had been in operation. In contemplating events of the next few years, the timing of this early experience seemed almost fateful.

For the second time, defects appeared in the rectifiers of Flotrol battery chargers. This time, however, they were discovered not during production, but after several hundred chargers had long been in use by customers. Chargers that had been working flawlessly for years began failing, first in a few locations, then across the country. The news came to Stocker as an echo of the 1937 Sub-Cycle nightmare, but his reaction was the same: identify the problem, find a solution, and replace the products, no matter what the cost.

Engineers quickly traced the trouble to the paint used on aluminum, which had replaced steel in the production of rectifier plates. After years of operation, paint on the warm plates softened, then gradually seeped underneath fingerlike pedal washers to break contacts and open circuits. A new combination of paint and metal produced the required resistance to heat, launching another crash program of machinery replacement, this one worldwide.

To accelerate the effort, Robert J. Pogorelc was appointed field service representative to assist Borer. A graduate of the National Radio School in Cleveland, Pogorelc had joined the company in 1951 as an assembler and advanced through the ranks to supervisor of the small Single-Phase Department. Over several months every rectifier identified as defective was replaced without charge at a combined cost of well over one million dollars.

"Our service reps went just about everywhere we had sold Flotrols in the past few years, except Cuba," said Chuck Ramaley. "Fidel Castro had just taken over the reins in that country, and he wouldn't let our men in, so we often wondered if anyone there figured out what went wrong."

While they were providing replacements, the two men also distributed sales literature, often obtaining orders for other products. "It's only a person like you who can take a bad experience like having a failure in a product and turn it into an asset by selling through servicemen," one customer told Stocker. Another wrote, "You are a master at turning a lemon into lemonade."

Service momentum thus gained during the exchange program continued when replacements were completed. Borer's Buick also was replaced with a company station wagon containing portable test equipment. Customers came to depend on Lorain Products servicemen to check equipment and make recommendations on upgrading facilities at telephone exchanges. "They knew that no one from this company would dare try to sell them something they didn't need," Pogorelc said. Many times when the servicemen returned from regular junkets, orders for new products already had arrived from companies they had visited.

The service representatives also organized seminars in several parts of the country, including Puerto Rico, to explain new equipment. These presentations brought invitations to present similar programs at sales conventions. Both were patterned after seminar courses held at the home office for customers interested in training maintenance men. When that program was initiated as two sessions in April 1958, response was so overwhelming that a third was scheduled later that month and plans were adopted to make it an annual event.

The telephone industry, at that time servicing 67,000,000

U. S. telephones through AT&T's gigantic Bell System and some 4,000 independent companies, prided itself on its widespread camaraderie. The U. S. Independent Telephone Association, in particular, promoted friendship and the exchange of ideas at its national conventions and those of its state organizations. By joining these groups, Lorain Products sales and service personnel became acquainted with representatives of equipment manufacturers (the company's primary customers) and end-users ranging from such large consolidated telephone companies as General Telephone & Electronics to the fascinating "mom and pop" small-town independents that still survived the pressures of dial-operated equipment and rising operational costs.

To improve the processing of incoming orders and tighten inventory controls, Lorain Products installed a combination of the Royal-McBee Keysort and Burroughs posting systems. Although Stocker hired an outside consultant to offer advice, it came as no surprise that he again placed more faith in recommendations of the company's own employees. "As so often happens," he explained, "it seems that we know our business better than people on the outside."

An unexpected nationwide recession, the third since World War II, had materialized near the end of 1957, making it necessary to intensify cash conservation efforts. Nevertheless, Stocker reaffirmed his conviction that capital investments should continue to hold a top priority. "The future condition of the corporation depends upon improvements to present products, the introduction of new products, and the expansion of facilities to properly handle present and future business," he told members of the board. He announced also that the engineering staff was being increased to "bring out a number of new items" in the next two years, and that a major wing would be added to Plant 3 in anticipation of expanded production. Backed by a balance sheet that remained strong, in spite of the recession, the company invested in short-term public bonds to assure availability of money for construction as programs progressed.

The extent of Stocker's optimism was dramatized uninten-

Cinderella and Closman Stocker and sons Paul (lower left), Doyle, and Glenn (standing), 1911.

Paul Stocker's high school graduation photograph.

Paul Stocker and classmate, Ted Root, at Ohio University, 1926.

Stocker and fellow Bell
Laboratories engineer in
New York City, 1928.

Paul Stocker works at his card-table workbench in the company's first laboratory.

Fred Heavens, co-founder of Lorain Products.

First Sub-Cycle advertisement appeared in the January 4, 1936 issue of *Telephony*
magazine.

Walter Krok, left, and Roland Smith work in the "cubbyhole" at 200 Seventh Street.

Dick Oldham, the company's first full-time employee.

The engineering group in 1953. From left, Paul Stocker, Jack Daly, Dick Van Deusen, Jim Goodell, George Pohm, Martin Huge, and Bill Christie.

The first company-owned building at 200 Seventh Street was purchased in 1937.

Entire work force posed for this picture in 1942. From left in front row, Paul Stocker, Walter Krok, Louis Paul, Dick Peters, June Oldham, and Evelyn Farschman. Behind them, Bob Kane, Dick Oldham, Bill Chapin, Martin Huge, Al Pfaff, Fred Heavens, Roland Smith, and George Pohm.

Employees and families attend 1944 company picnic at Stocker cabin.

F Street building before renovation.

Al Pfaff and Paul Stocker with early model of Sub-Cycle.

F Street building ready to be occupied in 1942.

tionally in the early stage of the $500,000 project, which began that fall.

Plans calling for an "addition" that in reality would be three times as large as the original building—approximately 40,000 square feet—were formulated by Jim Goodell, following consultations with Stocker, Huge, Pohm, and others, including Robert Woodward, vice president of the T. J. Hume Company. After final drawings were prepared by a Lorain Products draftsman, Ray Roth, trenching for footers was started even before Woodward could complete cost estimates.

While Goodell stood watching the trencher burrow along its course for the back-wall footer on a Friday afternoon, Woodward appeared with the cost figures. After looking them over, Goodell expressed surprise that the cost-per-foot charges were well below those for the construction two years earlier. "Maybe we ought to just keep on digging straight ahead, instead of turning the corner," he said, mostly in jest. "We'll probably be expanding again, so why not just finish the job now." Coincidentally, the trencher operator, Ed McElroy, chose that exact time to stop, dismount, and suggest, "You know, there is no sense in turning here; we'll be back next year putting on another addition. Why don't we just continue all the way down to G Street?"

As laughter faded into contemplation Goodell and Woodward headed for the main office where they presented the idea immediately to Stocker. Obviously intrigued, the president asked that they "work up some details" and bring them to his home by ten o'clock that night. Woodward always remembered that evening's meeting in exact detail:

> I made some hasty estimates, which Jim checked carefully, then we went to Mr. Stocker's home at the appointed time. He asked us if we wanted drinks, and we said yes, so he got us some iced tea. Then we discussed the idea and what it would cost. Next, Mr. Stocker telephoned Martin Huge and told him all about the proposal. Jim and I had no idea what Martin said, of

course, but when Mr. Stocker hung up the phone he ended the session quickly by simply telling us to move ahead with our plan. And that was it.

Trenching resumed the next morning, a Saturday, while Goodell and Roth began revisions of the design and drawings. "That's how flexible we were in those days," Goodell said. "Over a weekend we extended our thinking and our digging for another 30,000 square feet of factory."

When Al Pfaff arrived at work on Monday, he found Stocker standing at the construction site. Astonished to see what had been done, the production supervisor asked, "What in the world has happened?" With only the slight trace of a smile, Stocker replied, "We got that digger going and couldn't stop the damn thing when we came to the first corner."

Construction of the addition was made in three stages over the following year and a half. When completed, it almost doubled the space occupied by Lorain Products. Stocker kept in personal touch with the building's progress, even though he was busy with other affairs, including a final decision to move into Canada. Bob Woodward recalled a specific occasion when Stocker was observing construction:

He complimented the brick layer foreman on what a wonderful job his men were doing, going into detail about the alignments and mortar joints. When I came on the job, the foreman told me about it, and you would have thought he had received an award or a large amount of money. Mr. Stocker understood people's feelings. But he didn't do those things with an ulterior motive. Such a reason would never have crossed his mind. He was just that kind of a person. He made people feel good about themselves.

Stocker never hired architects during all the construction that followed, contending that they did not know the needs as well as his own colleagues (he never referred to them as his employees). Jim Goodell continued to design the structural steel work and interior layouts, with refinements added by the contractor, and Roth always prepared the final drawings. Woodward, a son-in-law of F. T. Hume (who had died in 1954 when construction of Plant 2 was in progress), started his own firm, Robert Woodward Construction Company, in 1960, at the age of thirty-five, and continued his association with Lorain Products in future projects. Time and materials were billed and paid regularly, without a contract, and a percentage was added at the conclusion as the builder's profit. "To have a man of Paul Stocker's intelligence and stature put that kind of faith in me meant everything," Woodward said. "How could you break a trust like that?"

The year 1958 would be remembered primarily as a time of major expansion. Yet, it was noteworthy in other areas also. In keeping with a national trend of the times, the company initiated a full major medical plan for all employees. And in keeping with his personal do-it-yourself philosophy, Paul Stocker bought a printing press, hired experienced printer Richard Schneider, and began in-house production of the company's manuals, advertising sheets, and brochures.

The new printing operation was supervised at first by Thelma Clark, who headed the company's Drafting and Blueprint departments. A graduate of Lorain High School who had advanced through production and drafting channels to her supervisory position, Clark also had served for several years as the company's only photographer. To enhance internal communication as the number of employees increased, she had started a company publication, the *Sine Wave*, in 1957. After appearing sporadically for a few years, it became a regular quarterly magazine, with employees in several areas of the company serving as editors, reporters, and artists. Schneider supervised its layout, printing, and publication.

EIGHT

EXPANSION

As America began climbing out of its recession in 1959, President Dwight D. Eisenhower disclosed plans for an economy drive aimed at swinging the federal budget from a deficit to a surplus. The business community expressed surprise at the speed of recovery, and the automobile industry, although (in the words of a *Business Week* writer) "befuddled by the reception accorded foreign cars whose designs change but slightly from year to year," enjoyed an upswing in sales. Worries about threatened steel strikes were offset by a rising rate of consumer income and new machinery orders, which combined to rekindle retail sales. Export sales also curved upward from the previous year's decline, but for many companies heavy tariffs made establishment of foreign subsidiaries seem preferable to shipping finished products across borders. Lorain Products fell into that category with respect to growing sales in Canada.

Stocker's interest in building a Canadian plant had become intensified, but he remained cautious. The company's sales in that country were extremely diversified, rather than concentrated on a limited number of products. This factor alone, he said, made it "difficult to reach a decision on the potential profitability of a Canadian facility." In addition, he was busy purchasing new properties that completed a solid block of company-owned land adjacent to the Lorain plants.

Encouragement to build a factory came from both the Canadian government and major customers such as British

Columbia Telephone Company, which strongly endorsed both the products and services of Lorain Products, but expressed an equally strong desire to buy commodities manufactured in its own country. With this backing, in May 1959 Stocker and Huge made an exploratory trip to St. Thomas, Ontario, where they met with bankers and the executive secretary of an industrial development corporation operated by that city.

Although the original intention was to locate a building for lease, each facility they visited was either too large, too small, or inadequately constructed for Lorain Products machinery. Consequently, they considered purchasing land for construction of a company-owned plant. After their return to Lorain, Stocker made a detailed report to directors:

> We drove out to see the industrial site which the St. Thomas Industrial Development Corporation had available. The Corporation is buying land from land owners around the city to reserve them for industrial sites. This is done to prevent the land from falling into the hands of speculators who hold it for higher prices and thereby prevent the development of a good industrial area.
>
> The Corporation had just received a deed for a very desirable piece of property the day before we arrived and they showed us this piece of land. The location was good, and the city was willing to put in the necessary sewer, fire hydrant, and other utility connections immediately to make it usable.
>
> . . . We met with [officers] of the Har-A-Mac Construction Company in St. Thomas. This company was highly recommended by the bank and the attorney as being a reliable firm. We discussed with them the problems connected with building on the site, and were told that they could operate on much the same basis as we now operate with the T. J. Hume Company.
>
> . . . The attorney was very definite in his feeling that we should retain an architect rather than attempt to deal directly with the contractor.

. . . Later in the afternoon we made final arrangements to buy a ten-acre site of land located on the corner of Edwards Street and Ontario Road. The purchase price coincides with the per-acre figure they paid for the land when they bought it.

On May 14, 1959, the second day of the investigative trip, Stocker signed a contract for purchase of the land. Three weeks later plans were announced to build the new plant at St. Thomas, eighteen miles south of London, Ontario. Designed primarily as an assembly plant at the outset, it was expected to grow into a manufacturing facility for "whatever products are in demand there," Stocker said. Har-a-Mac was awarded a construction contract for the one-story brick and block structure, but Stocker politely fended off further probes concerning his use of an architect. A few days later, Plant Engineer Jim Goodell arrived at St. Thomas to begin consultations with the contractors, who agreed to carry out the assignment on the company's preferred cost-plus basis.

While Goodell was designing the building and commuting regularly to supervise construction, three Canadians hired for key management jobs spent the summer months in training programs at Lorain. John A. McVeigh, named manager of the Canadian plant, had held a similar position with the St. Thomas works of Allis-Chalmers Company. Engineer John MacArthur was a former products engineer at Redman Motors, also in St. Thomas. Sales Manager Gerald Phillips had headed sales for Redman.

Construction was completed early in 1960 and on April 27 Lorain Products (Canada) Limited, the company's first wholly owned subsidiary, began shipping assembled units. For several months, all components were provided from the Lorain plants, but machinery subsequently was designed and built specifically for use in the Canadian plant, enabling the subsidiary to manufacture many complete products on its own. Expansions in 1961, 1967, and 1972 nearly quadrupled the plant's size.

Martin Huge, who had been with Stocker when papers were signed to consummate the purchase of property for the Canadian plant, had a special reason for remembering a brief celebration that took place later in the day. Gathering at the St. Thomas Country Club, a group including attorney Frank Sanders (who represented Lorain Products during the transactions), the mayor of St. Thomas, the city's industrial commissioner, a bank president, and other dignitaries toasted the occasion with highballs. "It was the only time I ever saw Paul Stocker take a drink of hard liquor," Huge said.

Although he might have one draft beer at a company picnic, Stocker saw "no redeeming qualities" in alcoholic beverages, and never felt uncomfortable in not serving them in his home. An admitted uneasiness at cocktail parties—he preferred being with family and close friends—was attributable more to a dislike for small talk than the presence of liquor, however, and he never evangelized on the subject of drinking.

Smoking, on the other hand, aroused his admonitory instincts. Having long ago given up his occasional pipe puffing, the company president felt obligated to help colleagues avoid the dangers of tobacco. His advice to smokers, personal and gentle in most instances, sometimes was punctuated with an original brand of humor designed to create a lasting impression. When employee Stanley Gaylord went to Stocker's office for a meeting one morning, he was startled to have a full pack of cigarettes pulled from his pocket. In a few swift motions, Stocker cut the pack in half with a razor-sharp knife he always carried. To each half he then attached one of his standard blue note sheets with the words "Stan's short smokes." Handing them to Gaylord as if he had done his friend a favor, Stocker suggested, "Just smoke one of these each time you have the urge for a cigarette and the pack will last you twice as long; that way you can save money and begin cutting down on your smoking."

A more calculated lesson awaited Robert L. Stephenson, a heavy smoker who was supervisor of accounting at that time.

In a brief informal ceremony soon to be reported via company grapevine throughout the plant, Stocker presented Stephenson a tailor-made white shirt with a single pocket placed almost inaccessibly over the small of the back. "Carry your cigarettes there and you won't be tempted so much," Stocker advised.

"I always had been careful not to smoke near Mr. Stocker," Stephenson said, "so it wasn't a matter of his being annoyed. He sincerely did not want his friends to damage their bodies by smoking. After he gave me that shirt, I didn't stop smoking completely, but I told myself that if he was willing to go to that extent, I wasn't going to smoke again at work. And I never did."

Stocker's concern for all who worked at Lorain Products compelled him to offer individual advice and assistance to such an extent that hundreds of employees had personal episodes to relate.

Philip Scagliozzo, who began as a young coil winder, went to Stocker for advice on purchasing a particular house, because his parents, "being from the old country," knew little about the city. After what Scagliozzo called a "question-and-answer period," Stocker said, "Let me do some research." The next day, he told the young employee he considered the proposed purchase "a good deal," then helped arrange a bank loan. Years later, when Scagliozzo had advanced through a chain of supervisory positions to manufacturing manager of the Transformer Division, he provided a composite of several other examples:

> I remember Mr. Stocker best for what he did for our people. When I was a supervisor, he called me many times asking how one of our employees was doing when he found out that person was sick. When people were hospitalized, he would ask if they were meeting their house payments or other financial obligations. He knew all about them. We were like a big family. After I answered his questions, problems would be solved in a

very low-key way. He didn't want any recognition, but I knew he did it. And he did it many, many times.

As head of the "big family," Stocker found many occasions to enlighten young employees on the values of thrift, something he practiced in his own life. Whenever an opportunity arose, he would expound privately on the importance of avoiding unnecessary personal expenses, investing wisely, and building savings accounts. Expensive automobiles in particular represented huge monthly payments at high interest rates—an extravagance he considered nonsensical. Spotting such an ostentatious object in the parking lot, he might trace its ownership to determine whether one of his young friends could use some fatherly advice on his favorite topic. If such a thing occurred, however, he never pursued the matter beyond offering an initial opinion; nor did he presume to render judgment. Rather, he would conclude, "If that is what you really want, you are right."

Stocker, who preferred economy cars for personal use, was the first person in Lorain to own a Volkswagen "Bug." He drove it to work and on trips and to pick up the president of the Bell Telephone System at Cleveland's Hopkins Airport. When he walked to the parking lot at the end of one work day, he discovered a huge, perfectly shaped wind-up key protruding from the Volkswagen's rear hood. Realizing by the quality of workmanship that the five-foot appendage was a product of company design engineers, Stocker made no mention of the prank. Instead, he drove the car for more than a week before removing the fabricated key.

"You would climb the mountain for a boss like that," said one of the perpetrators.

Employees were permitted to borrow tools and even company trucks for use at home, always on the honor system. Often when employees needed extra money for unanticipated expenses, Stocker would arrange overtime assignments, sometimes far afield from regular assignments. While working as a draftsman early in his career, Ray Young earned extra money running a drill press for two hours each evening. After later joining an assembly group, he was given an evening assignment helping document a building contract. (When Young told the president he was unhappy with a lack of good directions for preassembly operations, Stocker questioned him on details of his complaint, thought about them for a few days, then placed Young in charge of a newly formed assembly procedures department. The result was development of a visual instruction program praised by assembly workers, as well as the president.)

With such flexibility and close relationships continuing in the midst of growth, Stocker was troubled by rumblings of unionization occurring still softly but more frequently in the late fifties. In his estimation, strict union contracts would depersonalize the company's traditional method of operation and stymie employee opportunities for change and advancement. Nearly all employees at that time agreed.

————

By the end of the 1950s, America's industrial balloon was ascending on the combined currents of several recent technologies, any one of which could justifiably be considered momentous. Among them were nuclear reactors, computers, orbiting communication satellites, magnetic-core storage units, printed circuits, and transistors. All except the first directly influenced the continuing evolution of Lorain Products.

The transistor, a miniaturized marvel that replaced vacuum tubes and brought a 1956 Nobel prize to its Bell Laboratories inventors, was of special importance in the company's engineering research and development during that time. Its effect, in fact, could be measured in terms of new products introduced at the beginning of the next decade—one some historians would label the "age" of space, computerization, protest, or conglomerates, depending on the preferred frame of reference.

A new line of silicon rectifiers under the name Flotrol featured transistorized reference sources. At the same time, transistorized models of tone generators, ringing machines, carrier equipment, Bat-Tap voltage reducers, and DC to AC converters also were ready for the market. "So many new products were introduced during 1960 that at the U. S. Independent Telephone convention in Chicago we displayed a room full of equipment, with only one item from our old product line," Stocker said.

Equally important in the president's mind were two agreements with outside companies, which he predicted would have "far reaching effects on our business."

The first was a cross-license patent agreement, on a royalty basis, with the Western Electric Company. This agreement eliminated previous concerns over infringement of Bell System patents when both organizations were developing similar products, a situation that occurred frequently among groups seeking coinciding goals.

The other agreement involved patents assigned in 1936 by Lorain Products to the Automatic Electric Company of Chicago, an arm of the General Telephone System, covering the Sub-Cycle frequency converter and its improvement for use in foreign countries. When the Canadian subsidiary was established, Stocker discovered that six such patents still were active in that country. Considerable negotiation was necessary to cancel the earlier agreement, in effect buying back the patent rights, and one of the stipulations was appointment of Automatic Electric of Canada as the subsidiary's exclusive distributor for the entire country, excluding companies within the Canadian Bell System.

Intensified competition, spurred by record production, created a wave of price cutting across many industries, including those supplying the machinery for telephone communication. Stocker chose not to enter such a scuffle, considering it "a form of mutual throat cutting," and his company's record sales and net earnings in 1960 seemed to reinforce his evaluation. In addition to the expansions of Plant 3, the company remodeled Plant 1 and razed two small adjacent structures to make room for a large two-story wing.

When the new wing was completed in 1962, all manufacturing and assembly facilities for the first time were located in factories on the south side of the railroad tracks with Plant 1 devoted exclusively to administrative offices and engineering laboratories. The remodeled reception room, which utilized space as dividers to provide four relaxing areas for meetings with buyers, salesmen, and other visitors, received a top award from *Modern Office Procedures Magazine* and was featured in one of its issues.

One large basement room in the new wing was designed as a bomb shelter, reflecting strained international relations stemming from the 1960 Bay of Pigs Invasion, Russia shooting down a U. S. high-altitude reconnaissance plane, an increase in NATO forces, and construction of a concrete and barbed wire wall between East and West Berlin. When tensions eased, the shelter became known as "the auditorium" and was frequently used for seminars and meetings.

With the increased spread of facilities, Stocker ordered a pneumatic tube system to distribute interoffice messages throughout the growing company complex. After specialists were called in to bore a three-inch tunnel under the railroad tracks and G Street, the company from whom the tube system had been purchased began plans for its installation before they were stopped by the Lorain Products president, who explained, "We can do it ourselves." Describing how complicated the project would be, especially since it would go underground, as well as wind through and between buildings, the manufacturer wondered how an inexperienced group could handle such an undertaking. "Jim can do it." Stocker said confidently. And so it came to pass that a company maintenance crew did the installation, under the supervision of Jim Goodell, who read appropriate literature to acquire the necessary expertise. Goodell also sought and obtained the advice of George Pohm, the chief engineer described by nearly all employees as knowing "everything about everything." Accounting Supervisor Stephenson noted later that Stocker "just smiled his approval when the system worked perfectly, as he had known it would."

Stocker greatly enjoyed the increased administrative duties of the presidency as his company grew steadily in the early sixties. Yet, development of new products remained his pride, invention his passion. Hours spent in personal research dwindled, but never died. When he could not find time for hands-on participation in special projects, he always was available for consultation and encouragement. "Research engineers often told me Paul couldn't resist looking over their shoulders and offering suggestions," his wife said with a smile, "but none of them ever complained about it, at least not to me."

Western Electric, one of the company's most important customers, bought two types of equipment. Those identified by GA numbers were to be manufactured according to exact specifications established by Bell Laboratories designs. KS equipment also was expected to produce a precisely defined result, but design and development were left to the creativity of an engineering contractor. Stocker was interested only in the latter equipment. "Anyone who can follow directions can build GA machinery," he insisted, "but developing the circuitry and techniques to achieve a specific result is a challenge."

The soft-spoken president encouraged everyone in his organization to search always for improvement, whether it was in product development, manufacturing, or assembly, but he warned also of certain dangers in letting perfectionism become fanaticism. One young engineering genius could accept the most difficult assignments available and develop a high quality product. Yet he never was satisfied. "If it reached 97.5 percent efficiency, he didn't want to do anything with it until he reached 98.2 percent," one coworker said. Stocker patiently attempted to convince the young man that a product with efficiency well beyond requirements should be marketed, rather than held back indefinitely while edging toward an elusive perfection. Never quite successful in convincing the engineer of that reality, however, Stocker transferred him to another assignment whenever a suitable degree of quality was reached, and had other people move the product on into the manufacturing stage. "If Stocker hadn't done that," the same coworker observed, "the man might have worked on one project for the rest of his life."

Stocker had a high tolerance for eccentricities that did not interfere with the well-being of fellow employees or the company. Similarly, he never made judgments based on what he considered "artificial standards" that attempted to pigeonhole abilities according to personalities, physical attributes, and age. An example:

Mircea Petrini attempted to leave his native Hungary after it was taken over by Communists in the 1940s, but he was caught at the Austrian border and taken prisoner. Escaping later in a truck filled with bags of salt, he worked for a time in Vienna, moved to Brazil for nine years, then went to Canada, because the United States at that time would not accept immigrants born in Communist countries. After learning about Lorain Products in 1961 by selling the company some materials in Vancouver, Petrini wrote to Stocker asking for employment, explaining that he had been a factory manager in Hungary. Making special arrangements to prevent Petrini from becoming an illegal alien, Stocker invited him to Lorain for interviews with members of management. All went well, except that someone suggested Petrini, at fifty-seven, seemed too old for serious consideration. "But that makes him exactly my age," Stocker replied. "Are you saying I'm too old to be working?"

"Mike" Petrini was hired as a designer in the development group. Later, he standardized the design of a magnetic amplifier, enabling colleagues to save hundreds of hours in individual development. "Mr. Stocker followed my progress very closely," he said. "When he made a trip to Rumania, he got my sister's name, called her, visited the family, took pictures, and brought them back to me. I consider him my best friend."

An interesting epilogue to the Petrini story thoroughly squelched any thought of his being too old for productive employment. He retired in 1975, went to New York City "until congestion became unbearable" in 1982, then returned to Lorain. A year later, he was invited by Ben Norton, employee and community relations manager of Lorain Products (by then a division of Reliance Electric Company) and a son-in-law of Stocker, to rejoin the firm as a component specifications engineer. Petrini still held that position in 1989, at the age of eighty-five.

NINE

QUIET PERSUASION

In October 1957 Sputnik I, the earth's first artificial satellite, was launched as part of Soviet participation in the International Geophysical Year. This achievement was followed by two other Soviet satellite launchings in November 1957 and May 1958.

The impact of these events on American society created an enormous guilt complex, with particular injury to the nation's pride in its record of scientific leadership. "While we have been waging a war of automobile horsepower and talking about exotic fuels," said scientist Merrill F. Aukland, "the Russians have been making exotic fuels and talking about automotive horsepower."

Reactions to the situation were swift and intense. President Eisenhower appointed a committee to gather new momentum in space-related scientific achievement. An aroused public demanded examinations of the Department of Education, the National Science Foundation, colleges, and universities. Statistics were compiled to determine how many years it would take the United States to match the 55,000 engineers being graduated each year in the Soviet Union. Immediate changes in curricula, increasing the input of mathematics and appropriate sciences, were suggested for all levels of education. A coordinated effort by teachers, school administrators, industry, and statesmen was prescribed to dramatically increase the 2 percent of women college graduates earning degrees in mathematics, physical sciences, and engineering.

In Ohio, a twelve-member Commission on Education beyond the High School, which had undertaken its assignment from Governor C. William O'Neill six months before Sputnik, hastened its compilation of a "blueprint for the development of higher education in the state." Ohio University President John C. Baker, who served as chairman of the commission, insisted that anything approximating a crash program had been avoided carefully, although space-age concerns were among those that had prompted establishment of the group. Others, he pointed out, were aimed at extending higher education to all who had the ability and were willing to work for it, and to increase quality in all areas of study.

Among the commission's recommendations in the category of mathematics, science, and engineering were that "liberal arts colleges and divisions which do not have engineering schools should offer basic courses to provide for transfer to accredited engineering programs after two years," and that "two-year technical institutes should be established at industrial centers to provide suitable numbers of well-trained technicians to support engineering staffs." A closer association between higher education and industry was considered important in strengthening the nation's scientific competence.

While the report was being completed in mid-1958, a vacancy occurred on the Ohio University Board of Trustees. Before making an appointment to that important position, Governor O'Neill invited President Baker to recommend an alumnus who had been successful in building an industrial business, preferably in Northeastern Ohio. Baker, in turn, discussed several possibilities with his assistant, Brandon T. Grover, and it actually was Grover's wife, Gladys, who suggested the name of Paul Stocker. "Of course," Baker said, "he is just the man for the position, if he will take it."

Knowing about Stocker's modesty from brief meetings when the Lorain Products president served as an Alumni Association officer and received the association's Certificate of Merit in 1956, Baker realized some persuasion might be necessary. Consequently, he made an appointment to visit

- 103 -

the Stockers at their home. "During our very delightful chat, I explained that I could only make a recommendation, with no guarantee that the governor would appoint that person, but I would like very much to submit Paul's name as a candidate for trustee of Ohio University," Baker said. "His answer, however, was that he didn't have enough to offer, because he just stuck to business and didn't know the inner workings of a university."

Baker recalled that the conversation became one of his trying to convince Stocker of "the tremendous contribution a man with his knowledge and commitment could make to the university," and Stocker's "equally strong insistence that it would be wrong for him to be considered for appointment to a job for which he had no expertise," until a conversational stalemate was reached. What finally broke the impasse so intrigued Baker that he logged it in his diary:

> Beth Stocker, having listened patiently to the discussion, finally said, "Oh, Paul, let's do it. We'll learn something new." He looked at her and asked, "Do you really want me to? You will be involved with me." She said, "Yes, I'd like to do it with you." So he said, "All right, if the Governor chooses to appoint me, I'll do it."

Governor O'Neill made the seven-year Board of Trustees appointment a few days later, in July 1958. "I never was convinced that Paul would have said yes if his wife had not spoken up," Baker said, "so it always has been my opinion that she had a great deal to do with the strong interest he developed in Ohio University and the benefits that grew from it."

As a board member, Stocker was quiet and reserved. Not only did he listen, he also studied the embodiment of Ohio University administration and board responsibility. "He was a man with a lot of basic common sense and understanding, and when he spoke, his words were incisive," Baker said. "In the three years I worked with him until my retirement in 1961, I gained a lot of respect for his quiet strength and exceptional judgment. He didn't do anything with a casual curiosity. You could tell he had a genuine interest in the university and the education of young people."

Edwin L. Kennedy, a partner in Lehman Brothers who later served with Stocker on the Ohio University Board of Trustees, concurred. "Paul was very considerate of other people and concerned about their welfare," he said. "That came through very clearly. He only talked when he really had something of value to say. Yet, he was very personable, very likable. He also was a man of extremely high ethical standards. Those are the key impressions I have of him."

"My husband didn't believe in joining anything in an honorary capacity," Beth Stocker said. "When he was invited to be on the board of the National Bank of Lorain, he said he needed to learn more about the banking business and finance, so he studied those things diligently. Anything he did was considered a learning experience."

A prolific reader, Stocker was unable to skim books, explaining that he was too indoctrinated with the need for "word-by-word scrutiny" of business and scientific materials to simply peruse anything, fiction or nonfiction (his favorites were historical novels). When he became a director of the Lorain County Public Library, he kept informed on every aspect of its operations, even the selection of new volumes. He was equally involved as president of the Lorain Lions Club and as a member of the Lorain Community Concerts and Chamber of Commerce boards. He served as president of the Lake Erie chapter of the Society of Professional Engineers and as a director of that organization's Lorain County chapter. As chairman of a citizens' advisory group for the Lorain Public Schools, he worked assiduously with the superintendent and others on attaining high standards at a time when the nation's educational system was being severely criticized. On one memorable occasion in the late 1950s, he telephoned the school principal to mention that his youngest daughter, Mary Ann, was not being assigned enough home work.

"His expectations were very clear," Mary Ann said later. "School was our job, and it was not to be taken lightly. We were expected to do well."

Stocker became more directly involved in Ohio University academic affairs in 1961 when he accepted an appointment by Dean Edwin J. Taylor, Jr., to a Board of Visitors created within the College of Applied Sciences (changed in 1963 to the College of Engineering and Technology). Formation of the board was a response to the acknowledged need for closer liaison between education and the engineering profession.

In a magazine interview, Dean Taylor described the visiting committee, the first at the university, to be "an invaluable addition to the life of the college." As an example, he referred to committee input on preliminary plans that had been suggested for new engineering facilities. "These people are free from the usual internal pressures and politics," Dean Taylor said. "They are able to see more clearly the overall picture, and they do not hesitate to tell you about it."

(Ironically, committee members decided against the idea of locating a proposed combination engineering and science research center on the West Green campus, because they considered that area too confining for future growth. Other factors, primarily based on funding, forced the university to alter plans for its engineering-science complex, although it did construct a large science building that included space for electrical engineering, and two decades were to pass before new College of Engineering and Technology quarters would be constructed—on West Green.)

"Paul Stocker was an extraordinary gentleman," said Dean Taylor. "Our acquaintanceship grew into a close friendship, and I found that I could consult with him on the numerous problems we had in those days. He accepted chairmanship of the Visiting Committee, which included a fine group of prominent engineers, not all Ohio University alumni. Paul deserved credit for most of the things the group accomplished, because he was a working leader. I knew that whenever the University Board of Trustees was to meet, I could expect an early morning visit by Paul. He always drove to Athens the evening before the meeting and stayed at the university's guest house so he could come to see us in the morning before the board met. Paul Stocker learned everything about internal operations at Ohio University, as well as our college, and we always could count on having a strong voice on the Board of Trustees."

During this close relationship with the college, Stocker enjoyed meeting students, as well as engineering administrators and faculty members. Several students were invited to visit the plant in Lorain, and their teachers soon learned to recognize the characteristics Stocker considered basic to engineering professionalism: creativity, attention to details, a willingness to be critical of one's own designs, and high moral principles.

One of the students who attracted his attention was a senior named Pantelis "Pete" Paradissis, a native of Chios, Greece, who had traveled for a year as a merchant marine, then decided to study electrical engineering at Ohio University. By the time of his approaching graduation in June 1961, Paradissis had compiled an almost straight-A grade average, met and married student Beverly Ann Hafer, and made tentative plans to launch his engineering career in Boston. At Stocker's suggestion, he did, however, visit Lorain Products, where he received "a cordial welcome, a good interview, and a nice job proposal" from Vice President Huge on a day when the president was not there. Paradissis did not accept the offer, in fact, only because he and his wife still preferred moving to the East Coast.

Back at the campus about a week later, Paradissis answered a knock on the door of the prefabricated housing unit where he and his wife lived. The familiar visitor, who had attended a trustees meeting that afternoon, said, "Pete, I understand you turned us down." Admitting that was true, the surprised student agreed to talk about his decision. "Within a short period of time," he said, "Mr. Stocker convinced me that I would have a greater opportunity with his company, and as it turned out, he was right."

Paradissis began work that summer as a research and

development engineer for Lorain Products, living temporarily in one of the houses the company had purchased next to the plant. While advancing steadily through management levels, he brought his father, sister, and brother from Greece to Lorain. Not surprisingly, all received jobs with the company. "It was not unusual for Mr. Stocker to stop by on weekends and see how our family was getting along," Paradissis said.

———

Stocker was elected chairman of the Ohio University Board of Trustees in 1964, after serving as vice chairman during the previous academic year. Under President Vernon R. Alden, who had succeeded Dr. Baker in 1961, the university was beginning another period of physical and academic growth based on new educational concepts propounded by the National Defense Education Act and leaders of business and industry. Through a grant from the National Aeronautics and Space Administration, university engineers constructed and operated a "Radar Hill" facility to make lunar surface studies for the proposed Apollo moon shot. Modern language laboratories in a renovated classroom building were designed for group instruction and individual study. An advocate of a decentralized university, Alden emphasized development of branch campuses—organized under the Baker administration—to offer full four-year programs. The university also created a Center for International Programs, and all of its colleges were involved to some degree in summer training programs for Peace Corps volunteers. Alden himself was appointed by President Lyndon B. Johnson (who introduced his "war on poverty" program in a May 7, 1964 speech at the university) to head the Advisory Committee for the U.S. Job Corps. Alden recalled:

> I was intrigued that Paul and Beth Stocker would take really unusual, rugged trips abroad, but I think those trips gave Paul a very strong international out-

look so that he was a solid supporter of our efforts in Nigeria and subsequent projects in Vietnam, when we worked with the Ministry of Education in trying to develop a comprehensive educational system there. Also, he was chairman of the board when we invited President Johnson to talk at Ohio University. It was the first time a president in office had ever visited the campus, and his being a Democrat made the idea controversial, because the state government was Republican. Paul backed us completely although he also was a Republican. Later on we invited former President Eisenhower to the campus, and that provided a balance to the controversy.

Alden noted that Stocker again was "enormously supportive" when the university became involved in Appalachian development programs. "Being a practical businessman, Paul understood that southeastern Ohio was an underdeveloped area, and unless we had projects such as improving and expanding the highways, and even moving the Hocking River to avoid flooding, we could never have economic development," Alden explained. "We considered these things very important to the university, as well as the area, and Paul agreed, asserting himself quietly, but with great wisdom and experience, at board meetings and in private conversations with me."

President Alden's determination to elevate business education from what he considered "excellent training for entry level jobs" to "preparation for eventual leadership positions" brought "a tremendous hue and cry from the faculty and some students" in the College of Commerce (renamed the College of Business Administration). "That might have been difficult to ride out, if I had not had the support of Paul and such other board members as John Galbreath and Fred Johnson," Alden said. (It should be added that Johnson, a Columbus insurance executive, was the prime motivator behind the enormous task of moving the Hocking River from its natural course through the campus to a route circumventing Athens, thereby eliminating regular flooding that had plagued the city and university for decades.)

The university president also considered it an important measure of Paul and Beth Stocker's allegiance that they "showed up faithfully and continually at important events," making the two-hundred-mile drive from Lorain to attend receptions, lectures, and other programs to which trustees were invited. "Paul was not a part-time trustee," said Alden. "He was especially interested in engineering education, but he was very much involved in the whole fabric of the university."

When Lorain County Community College was chartered in 1963, Stocker was enthusiastic in his endorsement of its development. Opened for regular instruction at rented quarters in 1964, it became the first permanent state-aided institution of higher learning in the county, and the second public community college in Ohio. By the fall of 1966, the college had moved to a new 250-acre site, and in 1971 it received full accreditation by the North Central Association of Colleges and Schools. "Paul offered a lot of encouragement, and his company became a good industrial neighbor," recalled Dr. Omar L. Olson, president of the college from 1971 to 1986, before becoming executive director of the Ohio Technical and Community College Association. "We enjoyed excellent relations with Lorain Products, and the company hired many of our graduates."

Through a co-op program with Fenn College, students alternated three-month periods of studying on campus with similar stints as paid employees at Lorain Products. The arrangement was started on an informal basis in the 1950s; when openings occurred, either Stocker or Huge notified administrators at Fenn, who in turn recommended top students for interviews. The program was increased after Fenn College became Cleveland State University in 1964; assignments were made on a continuing basis, and several co-op students moved on to permanent positions with Lorain Products following their graduations.

At his own request, the company president received no

publicity when he provided a faculty enrichment fund for the Ohio University College of Engineering and Technology and made contributions to other educational institutions.

Stocker's personal encouragement for employees to seek educational opportunities expanded into a challenging incentive plan. Persons who enrolled in correspondence courses or attended night schools were reimbursed for total expenses, including books, as long as they maintained grades of A or B. The recompense was halved by a C average and eliminated by any grade below that level. The value of continuing education was expounded through company publications and direct conversations with the president, who was immensely gratified by each positive response.

"Like a lot of others, I always was enrolled in some kind of course, whether related to my work or not," said Dick McMillan. "One winter it was an advanced management course at Case Western Reserve every Friday night. Then I took basic computer and real estate appraisal courses at Lorain County Community College and even attended automobile mechanics classes at Lorain High School."

Ray Young attributed his eventual rise to the position of advertising manager, something he "never would have thought possible when I was a coil winder," to Stocker's insistence that he attend night school and get good grades.

"It would be impossible to guess how many people took educational courses in Lorain County because of Mr. Stocker," said Jim Jakubowski, another employee who enrolled in a wide variety of classes, all paid for by the company. "He was willing to help anybody who showed a real effort, and I don't think there ever were fewer than thirty employees at any given time getting educated because of his influence."

Employee Kenneth R. Bechtel had completed the equivalent of two and a half years of degree work in business at Kent State University's Elyria extension division when Stocker decided he showed exceptional promise for future management positions. Having reached the maximum academic level offered at the extension division, the young management trainee was investigating other arrangements for completion of a bachelor's degree until Stocker suggested that it would be "desirable" for him to "obtain a degree in the shortest possible time." To reach that goal, the president proposed a plan whereby Bechtel could attend Ohio University full-time "because of the outstanding courses in business administration offered there," and receive his degree in marketing. A stipend of $5,000 per year was offered, because Bechtel had a wife and three children. The only requirements were that the recipient should maintain a "B average or better" and agree to "come back to Lorain Products for a minimum of two years." Bechtel accepted the offer, returned to the company on schedule as manager of material control, and became customer service manager within a few years.

Stocker's educational interests were reflected also in his satisfaction that the company's own Power Seminars, headed by Sales Manager Chuck Ramaley, drew increasing numbers of participants each year. Enrollment swelled to approximately four hundred representatives of telephone companies and their suppliers from all areas of the Western Hemisphere. Three-day sessions, held twice each May, featured lectures by Lorain Products engineers conducted in the Plant 1 auditorium, and guided tours through research and manufacturing areas. Seminar manuals, providing minute details of power equipment, reached encyclopedic proportions. "The customer representatives who took part told us much of the seminars' popularity was attributed to having engineers leading the discussions, without any semblance of a promotional pitch," Ramaley said. In his traditional talk at each seminar banquet, Stocker also carefully avoided any sales message.

Continued training sessions at customer locations, arranged by district sales managers and conducted by service department personnel, ranged in length from two hours to two days. Custom-designed according to requests, they covered the installation, operation, maintenance, and adjustment of equipment manufactured by Lorain Products. As demand for such technical training grew, the company established service and maintenance schools in different sections of the country.

"You've often heard me say that education unlocks doors to personal achievement," Stocker once told a company supervisor. Then with a broader-than-usual smile, he patted the seminar manual and added, "Well, it doesn't hurt sales, either."

TEN

REACTING TO
CHANGE

Except for its effort during World War II, Lorain Products had avoided government work whenever possible through the first quarter century of its existence. "We simply were not set up to handle all the inspections and paper work required with such contracts," Stocker explained.

However, a large contract with Sylvania Electric Company, in connection with a very complicated power supply for the Air Force, erased the president's apprehension in 1962. Once his interest was aroused, he studied government procedures with his usual zeal and encouraged other management leaders to do the same. By the end of the year, the company had compiled a complete set of government specifications and established a department to handle the written parts descriptions, technical manuals, and other necessary paper work. Several engineers learned the intricacies of reliability factors, what made equipment acceptable for government agencies, and procedures in handling the changes necessary to meet government specificiations. Factory supervisors were taught to understand the requirements of government inspections.

"This was a costly education," Stocker wrote in a management memorandum, "but like all experience, it has to be paid for. It now is felt that we are in a substantially better position to carry on future work of this nature should the opportunity present itself. There is no reason why government-oriented business should not be encouraged to some extent and carried out to the limit of our abilities. It therefore is felt that government work may increase in the future."

Having laid the groundwork for substantial business expansion with new facilities and a greatly increased sales force, the company shifted into higher production. Sales increased nearly 24 percent in 1962, considered a recession year by most U. S. businesses. Profits suffered somewhat from large expenses in equipping a "heavy engineering" laboratory, but that facility also helped research engineers introduce new products, a process still considered by Stocker to be uppermost in determining the company's success.

"As rapidly as engineers can be hired and trained, we hope to increase our laboratory staff and facilities by from 25 to 35 percent per year," the president stated in a message to Secretary-Treasurer Roland Smith. "New products thus developed will contribute to the growth of the company and in turn increase the need for additional production facilities and higher inventories." Indeed, custom products—chiefly models of Flotrols—were designed during the year for Western Electric, New York Telephone, Southern Bell, General Telephone, and A. E. Laboratories, and new versions of previous products were introduced for general worldwide distribution.

Stocker considered entering the European Common Market by purchasing an interest in an Italian manufacturing company, but he tabled such plans when economic changes in that country made foreign investment less attractive.

With its fiscal posture seemingly more stable than at any time in the past, the company initiated something its president had wanted for many years—an employee pension plan. Combined with insurance coverage during employment, it guaranteed lifelong monthly payments following retirement. The Lorain Products Corporation Retirement Plan, financed totally by the company, became effective on December 1, 1962.

Another employee benefit plan, the long-established bonus system of distributing 15 percent of pretax company profits among employees, was highlighted at the end of each year in a ceremonial presentation presided over by Stocker. All employees gathered at a factory site for the event, and the president handed stacks of checks to supervisors, who in turn distributed them among coworkers. A brief, uncomplicated procedure in earlier years, the program became a large undertaking as employment expanded. Where he previously had stood at the center of a small gathering, Stocker now was forced to appear on a raised platform overlooking the large crowd. Because he still knew everyone's name, however, he was able to maintain the intimacy of the ritual, which always was concluded with a short talk on thrift.

Other messages covering a wide spectrum of subjects were communicated periodically by the company president over a public address system connecting all plant areas. Each employee received advanced notice to be prepared for these "PA announcements" that always opened with the words, "Attention please, attention please, this is Mr. Stocker speaking." At the sound of the familiar introduction, all employees ceased working to get information directly from their president on wages, benefits, upcoming projects, efficient use of time, new company policies, corporate finances, or even plans for the annual picnic.

At times, Stocker spoke candidly on controversial topics involving the national economy and probable effects on business, trusting employees to keep his remarks relatively confidential. On one such occasion, he prefaced his PA announcement by saying, "I will appreciate it if you do not discuss this too much outside your own families and attribute the observations to me, because the whole business community might feel that I have no business saying what I am about to say. I, on the other hand, take the position that we are all in this business together and if I can warn you so that some of you can benefit from what I say, this talk will be worthwhile." He then presented his analysis of current stock market fluctuations, federal economic policies, and business changes he anticipated in response to those indicators.

Insistent on maintaining "two-way lines of direct communication" with employees, Stocker was "absolutely astounded" to discover that laws of the 1960s prevented him from carrying out plans to form employee committees for regular discussions of problems. "To my way of thinking this is a simple matter of common sense," he said. Nevertheless, the company's Cleveland law firm informed him that a specific law forbade management to take an active part in establishing such committees. No amount of explanation could override his feeling of disbelief, a feeling he did not hesitate to express in one of his PA announcements.

———

In 1963, the company purchased more land adjacent to its factory area, as it prepared for more expansion. An IBM card-tabulating system was set up for inventory control and various types of indexing, as a forerunner to computerization. Innumerable engineering drawings kept in cabinets were transferred to microfilm. To begin a long process of introducing a new parts classification system, Richard Van Deusen, supervisor of the Specifications and Technical Writing Department, spent six weeks with the London, England, firm E. G. Brisch & Partners, developer of a complex, but highly efficient numbering method. When it was applied to Lorain Products requirements, the Brisch system enabled manufacturing personnel to locate immediately any of the more than eighteen thousand separate items in the company's stockrooms. In addition, research and development engineers could decode Brisch numbers to determine the shape, rating, and other data on any item, thus identifying parts similar to those needed for new designs. Members of the Specifications and Technical Writing Department worked with production, design, and engineering groups to assimilate and maintain current descriptions, identification numbers, and other appropriate data on all parts and products.

Canadian operations advanced markedly, as more products were manufactured there to decrease the volume of imports from Lorain. Resulting reductions in duty payments alone contributed substantially to the subsidiary's favorable earnings report. The building in Ontario was enlarged in 1963, but soon became crowded again, making further expansion imminent.

With computerization stimulating nearly all elements of the world's economic vitality, Stocker showed extreme interest in a project being carried out by a group of research and development engineers headed by Pete Paradissis. The objective was to perfect a product that could keep computers and other critical electronic equipment on line through sudden power outages. Without such protection, invaluable data could be obliterated by loss of electric power for even an instant.

In reading what others were doing to solve the problem, Stocker concluded that a small California-based company, Parametrics, appeared to be leading the field. Its all-electronic system, centered on a bank of batteries, was designed to take over—without the loss of a single cycle—when commercial power was interrupted. By "riding" the commercial AC line perfectly in phase with its frequency, the inverter unit could take over at the point of a power failure without interruption. The system was not absolutely reliable, but Stocker was sure it could be made to approach that goal. Certainly, he thought, it would fit well with what his own researchers were doing.

Stocker spent two days reviewing progress being made by Paradissis and concluded that a great deal of time and effort could be hurdled by purchasing Parametrics and using its knowledge as a base for further development. With that in mind, he asked Martin Huge to visit the Parametrics plant in Costa Mesa, thirty miles south of Los Angeles. What the vice president found was a Quonset-style factory with a manufacturing crew of fifteen persons, headed by an engineering genius, Robert S. "Stu" Jamieson, and by Paul E. Rolfes, an engineer whom Huge considered the preeminent businessman of the corporation. Both men expressed interest in selling Parametrics, pending approval of six other shareholders.

After receiving the report from Huge, Stocker flew to California for further inquiries. Two days later he returned to announce that a purchase agreement had been reached. "Just a matter of good horse trading," he explained to a company officer. Parametrics would operate as a wholly owned subsidiary, with Robert E. Johnson remaining as general manager, Jamieson as head of engineering, and Rolfes in charge of mechanical design and production. No immediate transfer of personnel from Ohio to California was contemplated.

Parametrics, organized in 1957 for the primary purpose of developing and manufacturing instruments for measurement and control, manufactured and marketed electronic gear for the military, but the "no-break" DC to AC inverter was the focus of Stocker's interest. In August 1963, all 10,000 shares of Parametrics capital stock were purchased for $450,000. The following year, eight applications for U. S. patents on key components and operating methods were transferred from Jamieson and Rolfes to Lorain Products Corporation, as engineers at both sites worked to get the single-phase power system up to Lorain Products standards of operating reliability. In the meantime, research was started on an advanced three-phase unit. The subsidiary's corporate structure was dissolved on October 16, 1964, and Parametrics became a division of Lorain Products.

Thomas W. Grasmehr, who had worked with the company as a co-op student while attending Fenn College and completed his doctorate in electrical engineering at Carnegie Institute of Technology (later Carnegie-Mellon), became director of research for Lorain Products in June 1965. After spending six months working in California with Jamieson on the three-phase inverter, Grasmehr returned to Lorain, assuming responsibility for complete operation of the system.

After the first three-phase unit was installed in Omaha, Nebraska, demands for fully developed systems put added pressure on production, which Grasmehr explained in the employee magazine, *Sine Wave*:

> The computer industry has a good reputation for delivering working equipment on schedule. Unfor-

tunately, standby power appears to have been the last thing to be considered in these real-time computer installations. Thus, we have received requests for a three-phase inverter system with very little time allowed for development and production of the new circuits involved. But if we wanted to get into this lucrative market for standby power, we had to accept the short delivery and produce the required equipment as soon as possible or lose the business entirely to other competitive products. The resulting short delivery time is why many of you have felt a good deal of pressure to get certain items for Parametrics.

Marketed under various trademarks, including ConstAC and GuardAC, the Parametrics products were used widely for large computers and process control systems of telecommunications and industrial customers. A newly patented Exchange Voltage Regulator (XVR), also produced by Parametrics, provided a constant voltage source for central office loads. These new product lines were particularly significant in opening major avenues of marketing for the first time outside the telephone field.

Technology's forward thrust also penetrated long-established areas of Lorain Products manufacturing. The first solid-state ringing and tone interrupters were marketed in the mid-1960s, and new Flotrol rectifiers using phase-controlled circuits for voltage regulation were soon to make magnetic units extinct.

———

Building 4, a 43,000-square-foot brick and concrete block structure was started in 1964 and completed the next year. The largest section, containing new baking ovens, vacuum impregnating and automatic coil-winding machines, and other state-of-the-art equipment, became new quarters for the Transformer Division. This move greatly increased production of transformers, but business grew so quickly that large quantities of those products soon were being purchased again from two outside sources.

A smaller second-floor area of the new facility was designed for the company's Graphic Arts Department, which had grown to substantial proportions and had recently added printed circuit board production.

Richard Schneider, who had owned a print shop before organizing Lorain Products' printing operation with a camera, a varityper and a ten-by-fourteen-inch sheet-fed press in 1958, remembered being "like a one-man band, serving as cameraman, platemaker, setup man, press operator, and bindery worker." Nine months later, he was joined by photographer Allen Pelton, who was hired by Stocker after serving four years in the Air Force and six years with U. S. Steel. Together, the two men developed printing, graphic arts, and silk screening to meet all the company's needs for publications and product identification. Within a few years, they were accumulating certificates and plaques from state-wide competition among full-scale printing organizations, including the top commercial shops. Four-color presses replaced the early equipment as Schneider supervised the printing and Pelton handled both the photography and darkroom processing chores. They also produced 16mm training films for employees. One of the motion pictures, "Work Smarter," prepared for Walter Glick, who organized programs on self-improvement, led to creation of an Idea Program, initiated in 1966 as an ongoing plan for employee suggestion awards.

"Mr. Stocker always told us, 'Do the best possible job you can, and I'll buy you anything you need to do it better,' " Schneider said. "We followed his advice, and always got the best equipment available, as long as we could document in advance what could be expected as a return on the invest-ment."

With the advent of printed circuit boards in the early 1960s, Schneider added a new dimension to his operations. The tie-in was natural. Graphic arts replaced wire assembly in elec-trical circuitry, and a first step in production was making a photo negative of the design. "I remember that Al and I made the first circuit board using a small tray and etching a sensitized copper plate with a two-inch paint brush," Schneider said.

When the company moved graphic arts into its newly constructed Plant 4, plans for mass printing of circuit boards were set in motion. Envisioning the next step as manufacturing the "raw" boards, as well as printing the circuits, Stocker soon established a Fabrication Department, followed by another group specializing in final assembly. With the complete operation being carried out in-house, Schneider said "an order for one hundred printed circuit boards would trigger the fabrication shop to make the raw boards, telling me to order appropriate transformers from downstairs, and move immediately forward to the finished product." Twenty years later that system of eliminating inventories, would be identified by the popular buzzword "just in time" production. "People thought of it as a fresh concept in the 1980s, but Mr. Stocker used it in the '60s," Schneider contended. "He just didn't give it a name."

Miniaturization of components led to progressively smaller printed circuitry during the next few years, and annual production surpassed a quarter million units.

———

In setting goals for the last half of the 1960s, Stocker placed a top priority on designing new equipment that would reduce the number of models to be carried in inventory and still meet all customer requirements. He especially hoped to manufacture a single line of Flotrol chargers, the company's largest revenue producer, by resolving engineering problems dealing with silicon-controlled rectifiers. Standardization of engineering designs and tightened performance requirements to improve reliability and reduce costs represented a second high priority.

With new employee benefit programs in place and confidence in continuing expansion of Lorain Products, the president hired Benjamin G. Norton to establish the company's first Personnel Department (after first working for six months in various departments to familiarize himself with what Stocker described as "the nature of the work and skills required for each job"). A graduate of Earlham College and the husband of Stocker's daughter, Jane, Norton previously worked in the industrial relations department of U. S. Steel's National Tube Division.

Still adament in his belief that excess levels of hierarchy worked counter to effective decision making in many corporations, Stocker intended to keep the structure simple and direct at Lorain Products. His door remained open to all employees, and he continued his "walk-around" method of management, greeting each person with a "Good morning," regardless of the time of day. When suggestions arose on changing the hours of working schedules, Stocker had employees select alternatives through a company-wide vote.

As before, the president always found time to instruct young employees in basic values. Carol McKinnon began working in the office during the summers of her high school years and continued to do so after entering Dyke College in Cleveland. Her home was less than two blocks from the plant, but arising early on summer mornings was not her natural inclination, so she found herself "dashing madly for Plant 1" nearly every day. In doing so, she had to pass under the window of Stocker's office. Consequently, she found the president waiting for her "on more than one occasion," to deliver a friendly, but "rather stern" talk on the importance of promptness. "He spoke to me as I'm sure he would to his own daughters," she said, "and I tried my best to improve, although it took a bit of time." After receiving her degree from Dyke, the young employee became secretary to Vice President Huge.

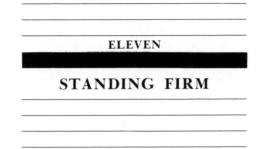

ELEVEN

STANDING FIRM

Paul Stocker was so imbued with the concept of his company as a family that any faint rumbling from organized labor reached shock wave proportions in his judgment. A confrontational separation between management and labor was unthinkable. It was a battle line between groups of friends —an unwelcome wedge that could shatter the foundation of equality and understanding on which he had built Lorain Products. The only benefits he could imagine would be for labor leaders, whom he considered self-serving intruders. Remaining free of their influence was more than a crusade. It was a fervor.

Murmurs of unionization during the company's accelerating growth in the early 1960s intensified, then surfaced in the summer of 1965 as a concentrated effort by the Communications Workers of America (CWA). Organizers arrived in the city to distribute literature among Lorain Products employees, talk to them before and after each work shift, and issue news releases to the media. Stocker countered with memoranda explaining his personal feelings and showing figures comparing the company's benefits with those being offered by the union. Vice President Huge and Robert Stephenson, then head of accounting, worked with the president in preparing the various presentations.

"Mr. Stocker was flabbergasted that any employee would even listen to the union representatives," Stephenson said. "He insisted the company's own programs were superior to those the union proposed, and we agreed with him."

Nevertheless, enough employees signed "authorization" cards indicating interest in union affiliation to bring the issue to a vote. In what was described by one employee as "one of the most traumatic experiences in the company's history," employees filed into Plant 3 on September 8, 1965 to cast their ballots at an election conducted by the National Labor Relations Board (NLRB). That afternoon President Stocker used the PA system to announce the results: Employees had rejected the CWA by a margin of two to one.

Philip Scagliozzo, then supervisor of the Coil Winding Department, happened to be nearby when the president bade a stern farewell to the union's outside organizers. "I had never heard Mr. Stocker speak an unkind word to anyone before that," Scagliozzo recalled, "but he made an exception in this instance, and I can remember word-for-word what he told those men. He pointed a finger at the entrance and said, 'There is the door; I don't ever want to see you again.' "

Because of Stocker's undisguised distaste for the entire experience, some employees who had signed cards were concerned about retribution. To allay such fears, Stocker assured them via the plant-wide PA system, "I'm sure that whichever side you were on, you felt justified in your position and voted accordingly." With that brief explanation, he said, "The election is over; let's turn to the work ahead."

On three occasions in subsequent years, unions tried unsuccessfully to obtain enough authorizations to meet Labor Board requirements for an election. The strongest of these attempts was made by the United Steelworkers of America, which sent a letter to Lorain Products seeking appointment as bargaining agent for employees, distributed handouts, and filed a petition with the NLRB requesting a secret election in 1971. Stocker replied in a letter to the union:

> This is in response to your letter of May 24, 1971, in which you allege that United Steelworkers of America has been designated as collective bargaining representative of production and maintenance employees of the company employed in our plants in Lorain, Ohio. You demand that the company recognize the union and

enter into negotiations with it as the representative of our employees.

The company rejects your demand because we do not believe that a majority of our employees in an appropriate unit wish to have your organizations represent them.

. . . You state in your letter that the union has filed a petition with the Labor Board. We believe that an election conducted by the Board is the appropriate means for determining whether or not our employees wish to be represented by a labor organization.

Although the union claimed in its literature to have the sympathy of a "vast majority" of employees, its experience in interviewing employees proved otherwise. In mid-June 1971, its petition to the NLRB for certification of representatives and the accompanying request for a secret election were withdrawn.

The U.S. commitment in Vietnam, which had begun with support of the anti-Communist Saigon regime in the 1950s and expanded to military involvement in 1961, escalated rapidly in 1966. Sorties into North Vietnam by B-52 bombers increased from sixty to eight hundred a month in what was code-named Operation Rolling Thunder, but the cost was high; 217 U. S. planes were shot down by North Vietnamese antiaircraft guns north of the 17th Parallel in little more than a year.

American troops doubled to 385,000, on the way to reaching a high of 536,100 in 1968, but Viet Cong men and supplies continued to flow south along the Ho Chi Minh Trail. Although coastal areas were kept relatively secure by navy vessels and planes, South Vietnam's Saigonese army had difficulty holding captured interior territory whenever U. S. troops pulled out. Criticism by doves, who wanted to cut back on the war effort, was matched by that of hawks, who insisted on a greater military action.

President Lyndon B. Johnson, convinced by his military advisers that heavier bombing would bring North Vietnam to the bargaining table, requested a 10 percent income tax surcharge to finance the war, and called for increased manufacturing of military products.

The resulting government priorities for the war campaign made it difficult for Lorain Products to procure some of its vital raw materials, especially copper, and many component parts. Lead time for obtaining such materials grew to as much as six months, making it impossible for the Sales Department to guarantee specific delivery dates. Consequently, at a time when the company was enjoying increased demands for its products, a growing backlog prompted Stocker to call 1966 "the most difficult operating year in our recent history." Sales, however, showed a 9 percent gain, and a slight decrease in profits was attributed only to raises in wages and fringe benefits.

New products continued to be introduced at both Lorain and the Parametric Division in Costa Mesa. Most notable were a DC-operated fluorescent lamp for stand-by use (with a trade name of FluorAC), a "programmed charge-discharge unit" for automatically determining the remaining useful life of a battery, a new line of exchange voltage regulators, and an all-solid-state ringing installation. The manufacture of complete power assemblies, or power boards, also represented a rapidly growing segment of the company's business.

Roland L. Smith, the first employee hired by the company's cofounders, retired at the beginning of 1967. He was succeeded as secretary-treasurer and board member by Robert Stephenson. A native of Lorain, Stephenson had worked for U. S. Steel before joining the company as an accountant in 1954. He had been promoted to supervisor of the Accounting Department in 1960.

An in-depth analysis of operations brought a series of concrete proposals for changes aimed at increasing overall efficiency in 1967. Every department in the company participated, with all employees invited to offer suggestions. Changes in factory procedures smoothed the flow of production. Several small assembly departments were combined. Test facilities were relocated and joined into a central testing area. Circuit board etching, fabrication, and assembly became a single department. Floor plans were redesigned, and new construction expanded work areas in the California and Ontario plants. Based primarily on the success of these concentrated efficiency measures, profits increased 42 percent while sales went up only 10 percent, prompting Stocker to move forward with expansion once again into what he confidently predicted to be "another new era of achievement."

That "era" began appropriately with the Lorain Products president being named Engineer of the Year by the Lorain County Society of Professional Engineers, at its February 1968 annual meeting.

Construction of a 40,000-square-foot addition doubled the size of Plant 4 in mid-1968, providing for steadily increasing production of transformers and printed circuits. At the same time, the company purchased an existing garage-style building adjacent to Plant 2 for vehicle maintenance and storage.

While the company was in the midst of its latest physical expansion, Stocker was making plans to extend product lines through an arrangement that required a philosophical alteration in his style of management. The reasoning for such a change focused on his faith in the potential of an electrical engineer who had been employed for the past seven years by the Rural Electrification Administration (REA) in Washington, D.C.

William Chambers was a tall, powerful former football player at the University of Florida. After graduation in 1960, he had joined the REA in its Telephone Standards Division, where he became a specialist in station equipment, ringing systems, and electrical protection of equipment. He also gained a background in system design and transmission. But REA was an administrative organization, as the name implies, and Bill Chambers was eager to enter an entrepreneurial field where his ingenuity could help advance the telephone industry. Knowing Martin Huge from frequent professional contacts with Lorain Products, he approached the company's vice president with a proposal that he be hired on an incentive basis, receiving a share of profits generated from his own inventions. Huge anticipated correctly that Stocker would be apprehensive, but he was sufficiently interested in specific product developments propounded by Chambers to discuss them with the president. After weighing probable dangers in making an exception to previous policies, Stocker agreed to the incentive arrangement, although any Chambers patents—like those of the other engineers—would become the property of the company.

Beginning as an engineer reporting to Brian Howald in March 1968, Chambers worked first on development of a solid-state party line telephone privacy device he had invented in 1966. Soon afterward, however, he was given the title of product manager, with considerable latitude in making decisions on design and manufacturing of new lines involving his previous patents, now assigned to the company. Most prominent were those for a loop extender and a companion product, the voice frequency repeater.

Telephone companies showed special interest in the loop extender, which promised large financial savings by gaining efficiencies in boosting signals for distant subscribers. Existing systems required progressively heavier cables as distances increased from the telephone central headquarters. Loop extenders developed by Chambers and other Lorain Products engineers working with him solved this problem by providing slight changes of voltage in proportion to the distance of transmission. The voice frequency repeater provided amplification on lines requiring loop extenders. These and other products created under the guidance of Chambers soon became major sources of company income.

Stocker was well aware of what he termed "some confusion" concerning the only product managerial position in the company, but his diplomacy overcame this small amount of grousing, which he considered inevitable and understandable. An obviously determined Chambers, also mindful of individual resentments, considered his challenge "a clear-cut opportunity to fail or succeed," adding that playing big-time college football taught him "you either win or get carried out on your shield."

At the same time the loop extenders and repeaters were broadening company manufacturing beyond conventional product lines, Stocker reported that development of the Uninterruptible Power System (UPS) had proved to be "a major engineering breakthrough." Based on a "traditional" principle of products dating back to the company's founding, the UPS was advertised as featuring a static method of providing continuous AC power with "no moving parts to wear out or break down."

During final stages of perfecting the UPS, Stocker made "a very difficult decision" to move the Parametrics Division from Costa Mesa to Lorain, after concluding that "we can manufacture Parametrics products at a great reduction in cost at Lorain." His decision, confirmed by the other three board members (Huge, Stephenson, and Beth Stocker), was based on lengthy studies culminated by an extended visit to the California subsidiary by Ken Bechtel to review operations and make recommendations. The timing was based on expiration of a five-year contract agreed on at the time Parametrics was purchased.

On January 15, 1969 the Parametrics Division discontinued operations. Selected employees wanting to transfer to Lorain were offered relocation expenses, but only three chose to leave the West Coast. One of them, Office Manager Norma Berrier, was the last person to leave the California plant, locking the door and giving the key to the landlord, then heading for Lorain, where she later became the company credit manager. Inventories, drawings, and plant equipment were shipped to Plant 4, and manufacture of the full Parametrics line of inverters was underway within a few weeks.

During the time of the move, the company's first full installation of a UPS system was made for the New Jersey Bell Telephone Company at Newark, supplying power to an IBM 360 System Computer used for intercept service.

A year later a Lorain Products UPS system put into operation at Minneapolis became the largest single assemblage of equipment produced to that date by the company. The complex unit assured uninterrupted power to computers carrying the entire reservations system, flight information, payroll, and inventory for North Central Airlines. Tailoring it for that specific use required an almost total mechanical redesign of the earlier unit by Project Engineer Robert Plow, with the support of others in the Engineering Department. William Dancik was in charge of production of the equipment, and Phil Smith spent nearly five months in Minneapolis supervising installation. Ten departments were involved in total preparation of the system, providing what the company described as ample justification for the transfer of Parametrics operations from California.

Later, UPS systems were installed at the White House to guarantee uninterruptible service of the presidential "hot line" to Russia, at military installations across the country, and at telephone companies serving major metropolitan areas. "In those days, every time an elevator went up or down there was a drop of electrical power that could cause problems for computers," said Production Coordinator Al Pfaff, "so production of our whole line of UPS units came into demand for those uses and others, including TV transmission."

A proliferation of electronics industries, coupled with continuation of the war in Vietnam, made competition for materials increasingly intense near the end of the 1960s. As a consequence, Pfaff, who had dealt with suppliers and inspectors for many years, was given a new assignment as expeditor. Working closely with the Purchasing Department to identify critical needs, he traveled throughout the country on what he referred to as "arm-twisting missions." In many instances, his entry was enhanced by long-standing friendships with former salesmen who had advanced to high management positions. One experience of special note was recalled by the Lorain Products veteran as typical of several such incidents:

I remember going to an East Coast supplier whose demand exceeded production of components important to our company and many others. Telephone calls and telegrams had failed to get us sufficient parts, so I made an appointment and stopped in to visit a contact person there. In the course of the conversation, I asked him about a salesman I had dealt with many years earlier, and was told that the man now was president of the company. When I explained that we were old friends, the man called the president's office to give him my name and company. Within five minutes, I was sitting with the president talking over old times. Then, when he asked me why I was there, I told him we were having a little problem with some deliveries on critical orders for capacitors. He told me about the company's trouble with demand outstripping supply, but asked, "How many do you need, Al?" I replied that we needed two hundred, but half that amount would get us out of immediate danger. With that, he called someone on the telephone and told him to "divert" one hundred of the components, "and give them to Al." I took them home with me that afternoon.

Pfaff attributed much of the success in expediting to Stocker's firm stand on always treating suppliers as fairly as if they were customers, paying bills ahead of deadlines, and maintaining good personal relationships.

Being courteous to representatives of suppliers, however, did not imply that the Lorain Products president would sacrifice his stance against wasting time. Salesmen learned to make presentations brief after discovering that their tenure in Stocker's office was controlled by the same timer used for in-house meetings. When the alarm sounded at the end of an assigned number of minutes, the session was ended.

Stocker was no less time conscious in business negotiations with executives of other companies. The president of one large firm began an out-of-town breakfast meeting by talking about his horses, knowing that Stocker had grown up on a farm and thereby assuming he could ease into the topic at hand with some introductory small talk. Responding as politely as possible, Stocker said, "We really don't have time to discuss horses. My colleagues and I have to get back to Lorain. Tell us what kind of deal you are proposing."

An executive of another company arrived at Stocker's office carrying an instant-developing camera before that concept had been introduced to the public. During business discussions, he took photographs of the assembled group, laying the finished prints on the coffee table for all to see. When negotiating bogged down after a brief time, however, Stocker glanced quickly at the photographs, and said, "I think your pictures are very nice, but the meeting is over, so I guess it is time for you to take your camera and leave." Rob Stephenson, who was in the group, remembered, "Mr. Stocker made the statement so humorously that there were no hard feelings, but there also was no question that negotiations were ended."

The incident was particulary noteworthy in exemplifying the value Stocker placed on time conservation when compared with his fervent interest in photography. An expert photographer, he often presented slide shows of worldwide trips at company parties, and his color prints and transparencies were noted for their professional composition and technical quality. "Buying the best available cameras probably was his only personal extravagance," a close friend observed.

Although America's infatuation with computers sparked rapid growth in sales of UPS and related products, computerization of operations within the company itself evolved slowly. Stocker saw no irony in that comparison, and indeed acknowledged the eventual indispensability of computers, but he was aware also of what he considered overkill by companies rushing to put the electronic marvels into superfluous uses. Rather than having them as "status symbols in offices where they were not even cost-effective," he contended, it would be more reasonable to give precedence to manufacturing. Increasing production offered a greater incentive to computerize than altering an accounting system that already worked quite satisfactorily. Consequently, the first full-system computer installation at Lorain Products was developed for inventory control.

Programming the computer to incorporate the Brisch number system and other complexities of inventory control became a team function. Soon after it went on line, Charles Scanlan, whose brief experience was in the Systems Procedures Department, became supervisor of computer operations. Scanlan had worked part-time while studying data processing at Lorain County Community College and had joined the company after graduation in 1967.

Meeting this new responsibility required frequent sixteen-hour working days and an understanding wife for the recently married young supervisor. "We lived nearby, so my wife would bring dinner to the plant and we would eat together in one of the rooms," Scanlan said. "I never mentioned it to Mr. Stocker, but one evening he came in and found us eating. He was extremely impressed that she would go to that trouble, and it bothered him that I had to work so hard. In fact, he was more concerned about that than about details of the computer operation."

Scanlan's observation correctly reflected the president's attitude toward computers. He was vitally interested in what they could accomplish and how they would be applied to more operations in the future, but he never studied their inner workings nor looked over the shoulders of operators. For reasons he never revealed, the compelling curiosity Stocker exhibited for every other machine and product seemed not to spill over into computers.

TWELVE

INTERNATIONAL
OUTLOOK

Under the leadership of President Gustavo Diaz Ordaz, Mexican industry and agriculture grew in the late 1960s. International credit was strong, the peso was stable, and factories springing up at an unprecedented rate gave Mexico City its first experience with the unmistakable symbol of industrialization—smog.

Foreign investment remained the backbone of the nation's industrial expansion, but the Mexican government was determined to eliminate what it considered former exploitation by U. S. businesses. President Diaz Ordaz, whose mutual friendship with U. S. President Lyndon Johnson received headlines in both countries, hoped to strike a balance between encouraging participation by U. S. industries and avoiding their economic domination. Under terms of a Border Industrialization Program established in 1964, certain wholly owned U. S. companies and subsidiaries in northern Mexico could import raw materials duty-free if all finished products were exported. In other instances, a more recent Mexicanization policy aimed toward eventual self-sufficiency required a flexible percentage of Mexican ownership, depending on competition, local employment, and decisions to locate in areas needing new industry. Private investment was on the rise, but the government still controlled the electricity, railroad, and petroleum industries.

Expanding and improving the nation's communication

system was the dominant objective of the nation's only telephone company, Telephonos de Mexico, popularly referred to as TELMEX, also controlled by the government.

Growth of Lorain Products Corporation's export business to Mexico essentially paralleled TELMEX maturation, although products serving nontelephone markets also were expected to gain wide acceptance there. Roy Head, the company's district sales manager headquartered at Denton, Texas, was spending an increasing amount of time in Mexico City, promoting various product lines, all of which were actually sold through a distribution arrangement with International Telephone & Telegraph Corporation.

By 1968 the volume of business with Mexico, coupled with promising forecasts by company planners, encouraged President Stocker to contemplate launching a manufacturing subsidiary in that country. Equally motivating were well-substantiated reports that the Mexican government hoped to bolster its economy further by insisting that continued marketing be tied to production within its borders. Stocker interpreted that to mean a competitor could open a plant in that country, then pressure the government to give it exclusive marketing rights. The obvious answer was to get there first.

In late June 1968 Stocker made an investigative trip to Mexico, calling upon ITT representative Carlos Silva to help him look for possible plant sites and contact persons who could give authoritative answers to basic questions of feasibility and legality. One of the most critical ambiguities was the percentage of Mexican ownership required of a foreign-owned company serving communication markets; opinions ranged from zero to more than 50 percent.

Stocker was unable to acquire an immediate judgment on that topic, but he did receive a thorough indoctrination into the industrial, marketing, and political workings of the country. He also toured facilities of prospective suppliers and drove to possible plant sites ranging from newly established industrial parks in Mexico City to a small town offering tax incentives and long-term options pending government approval on application for establishing an industry. Finding nothing satisfactory for lease, as he had hoped, he returned to Lorain with the thought that it would be necessary to buy land and construct a factory.

Plans progressed slowly through further exploratory phases for a year, while more immediate affairs transpired, such as completing the Parametrics move, building Plant 4, and introducing a new line of products. A specific proposal was prepared, however, and Stocker personally inspected early construction of a building slated to be offered for lease in Naucalpan de Juárez, a suburb of Mexico City. Jack McVeigh, general manager of the Canadian subsidiary, was enlisted to take part in the project, and when he accompanied Vice President Huge to Mexico City in the summer of 1969, it was with the intention of expediting plans for the earliest possible implementation.

Meeting with Luis Bravo, director of industry at the Mexican Ministry of Commerce and Industry, Huge and McVeigh explained the history of Lorain Products business in that country, and how it expected to hire workers there, as well as improve service to TELMEX. Bravo raised no objection to the plan, assuring his visitors that their company would be allowed to import any products not being manufactured in Mexico. He also expressed the hope that the company would have a successful operation and benefit the community. Borders would be closed to imports of any items manufactured there by Lorain Products, he said, but he requested a list showing the percentage of Mexican-made components and a plan for increasing the integration of more such parts in forthcoming years. No conclusion was offered, however, on the extent of Mexican ownership that would be required. Consequently, that uncertainty remained an enigma that lingered for many months, long after the subsidiary, Productos Lorain de Mexico, S.A. de C.V, was ready for production.

Although Jack McVeigh agreed to move from the plant in St. Thomas, Ontario, for at least six months to direct the establishment of Mexican operations, it was imperative that the company recruit a permanent general manager. Several men at the home office were capable of filling that position, but none had the necessary Mexican background. So a search began.

While Huge was compiling a list of candidates submitted by the Chamber of Commerce in Mexico City, Roy Head, on a sales trip to that area, noticed an intriguing classified advertisement in the English-language newspaper. Appearing in the Job Wanted column, it listed the experience and desire for employment of an electrical engineer named Noel Trailor. "Just on a hunch," Head sent a clipping of the ad to Huge, along with a note reading, "You might want to talk with this fellow." Huge in turn put Trainor's name on his list and invited him to the interviewing sessions being held in Mexico City. "I'm certainly glad that chain of events happened," Huge said later. "When we [he and Stocker] interviewed the candidates a week or so later, only one person had the qualifications we needed, and that man was Noel Trainor."

Born in Northern Ireland, Trainor received his engineering degree at the Belfast College of Technology. Not wanting to pursue his career in the atmosphere of murder and rioting that seemed never to end in his native land, however, he joined his brother in moving to Mexico, where they married sisters of a prominent family. While establishing permanent residency in that country, Trainor worked with a Westinghouse subsidiary in Mexico City and as chief electrical engineer for Celenase Mexicana, before placing the newspaper advertisement that brought him to the attention of Lorain Products.

In September 1969 McVeigh moved to Mexico City, with John MacArthur taking charge of the Canadian subsidiary during his absence. Jim Goodell arrived to install machinery and assist in setting up operations at the leased facility, which was the approximate size of Plant 2 (13,000 square feet). Robert Magdaleno, a member of the Service Department in Lorain, was assigned to the Naucalpan plant to establish quality controls and field services. Trainor was sent to Lorain and St. Thomas for extensive training, before joining the management group in Mexico. He became general director in late 1969, and McVeigh returned to his position as head of the Canadian subsidiary.

Stocker's direct leadership in establishing the Mexican subsidiary was shelved temporarily in the summer of 1969 when he suffered a heart attack. This setback at the age of sixty-five was the first since a minor operation in his youth. Always vigorous and in good health, he rarely had missed a day's work because of illness, and from the moment he began to recover in the hospital, his thoughts were on getting back to family and company as soon as possible. However, he had such faith in employees that he did not worry about progress of the business. Doctors attributed his heart attack to overwork, a conclusion he reluctantly accepted even though he never really thought of his activities with Lorain Products as being a separate part of his life.

Recuperating at home by August, Stocker resumed writing a regular presidential column for the employee publication, the *Sine Wave*, expressing his gratitude for "your good wishes and prayers, which played a large part in my recovery," and his confidence in the quality of work being carried out at the plants.

Stocker's daughter, Jane Norton, recalled that her father did what the doctor suggested during recovery, "except that he anticipated, rather than followed orders." When the doctor told him he was ready to walk "a couple of miles a day," the patient already was on a five-mile schedule. Soon afterward, he resumed one of his favorite exercises, splitting wood. Then he asked the physician if it would be all right to engage in that activity. "I think I would hold off on wood splitting for a while," the doctor said, at which point Stocker confessed he had been doing it for two weeks. "Well, if it hasn't hurt you by now, I guess it's okay to continue," was the reply.

By fall, the president was back at work, at first part-time, then on a daily schedule. There had been no interruption of administrative functions, attributable at least in part to the fact that Stocker always confided in Vice President Huge on top-level matters.

———

With a skeleton staff ready to hire personnel and begin manufacturing operations, unanticipated delays postponed opening Productos Lorain de Mexico for more than a year. Approval of the Ministry of Commerce and Industry was required for each of the proposed products to be built or assembled at the plant: ringing generators, static inverters, DC to DC converters, combination power units, power boards, and solid-state interrupters. Authorization had to be arranged for importing all machinery, equipment, raw materials, and parts. Detailed projections were required for short- and long-term "integration" of Mexican-built components. Guaranteed standards of quality had to be documented in exact accordance with specifications established by the government's general director of electricity. Noncompliance could bring "cancellation of all applications for important permits required by your company."

After a series of negotiations, the minimum for Mexican ownership of the subsidiary corporation's stock at last was set at 40 percent. This requirement presented a difficult obstacle for Stocker for several reasons. As a relatively small company compared with the industrial giants most prominently represented in Mexico, Lorain Products was not positioned well to sell stock on a general market. The only people who really wanted to buy it, Huge reported, were "competitors motivated by thoughts of gaining control." Some private entrepreneurs offered to purchase the necessary stock, but with stipulations unacceptable to Stocker. Others with available cash and sufficient interest in the company lacked the required citizenship. Schemes proposed by one group reflected an obvious ignorance of the president's morality (he defined them as "subterfuge"). Banks would invest only if they could have controlling interest.

Showing his characteristic calm amidst a crisis, Stocker

told Secretary-Treasurer Stephenson, "We really have to give some thought to this." In the brainstorming session that followed, Stephenson remembered that an uncle of his son's fiancé was a physician near Mexico City. A Mexican citizen, the doctor had met and married his wife, who was from Lorain, while interning at a Texas hospital. If he became an investor, Stephenson suggested, there should be no worry about ulterior motives.

Dr. Gustavo de Echavarri indeed was interested, and when Stocker visited him in Mexico, the two men sensed an immediate rapport. His subsequent investment, plus shares purchased by Noel Trainor's wife, Kokis, and by the father of the subsidiary's general accountant, Rafael Topete, met the percentage requirement. (The personal friendship between Stocker and Echavarri subsequently became so close that the Mexican doctor often flew to Lorain for company or family social events, including the wedding of his niece and Stephenson's son.)

Funds borrowed from the parent company provided additional financing for capitalization of the new subsidiary. Production did not begin until early 1971, but within two years it almost equaled that of the Canadian subsidiary, even though the latter was advancing steadily.

With production well underway in mid-1971, Robert Pogorelc was reassigned from his job as assistant production manager at Lorain to a one-year tour of duty at Productos Lorain de Mexico. Coordinating his effort with Production Manager José Mario Lopez and Sales and Service Manager Saul Arrazola, Pogorelc traveled to widespread areas of the country, making arrangements to acquire raw materials and components from Mexican suppliers, and helping develop the Service Department. "For most of that year, I was a one-man field service team," he recalled. Under terms of an escalation clause in the Ministry of Commerce and Industry agreement, integration of Mexican-made parts was expected to increase by 40 percent within a year. Fortunately, that schedule was met, and a second 13,000-square-foot building was leased as the first production year ended.

When Pogorelc returned to Lorain, he was asked by Stocker to form the company's first International Department, with assistance from Jack Wagner, who had provided liaison from the home office during his year in Mexico, and secretary Tanya Zaber. The three-member department, reporting to Secretary-Treasurer Stephenson (who was responsible for all international activities), was destined to grow substantially as the company's worldwide sales and affiliations expanded during the next few years.

The plant in St. Thomas, Ontario, having been expanded in 1961 and again in 1967, manufactured a full line of company products, with nearly all parts being purchased in Canada. All seventy of its employees in 1971 were Canadians, many of whom had been trained at Lorain plants. Another major addition planned for 1972 would increase the plant's size to more than 46,000 square feet, three and a half times that of the original building constructed thirteen years earlier, and provided for a 20 percent increase in employment.

––––

While extending its international peripheries, the company had constructed a metal fabrication shop and finished-goods warehouse addition to Plant 3 in 1969 and purchased two existing buildings adjacent to its manufacturing complex. These buildings, plants 5 and 6, were used for various manufacturing facilities and the Service and Repair Department.

In 1972, with employment exceeding a thousand at Lorain, the company began what proved to be the last construction under Stocker's ownership. The *Lorain Journal* made this report:

> Lorain Products Corporation, designers and manufacturers of power equipment for communications and industry, is taking another giant step in its phenomenal growth with a new $750,000 addition to its main building at 1122 F Street on Lorain's East Side.
>
> "Faith in the economy of our nation, the future of Lorain, and in a demand for our products form a com-

bination of reasons for our expansion programs," said C. Paul Stocker, president of the personally held corporation.

The new two-story brick and steel addition, with 30,000 square feet of space, is going up on the west end of Plant 1, occupied by the executive and administrative groups, research and engineering, library, computer terminal, and the sales, design, and business service departments.

. . . Company plants are located on both sides of the Norfolk & Western Railway tracks, west of Kansas Avenue, and have a total of nearly 350,000 square feet of space in buildings on 21.6 acres of land.

Stocker said the new addition will have a tunnel under the N&W tracks, which will make it possible to truck heavy equipment from the south side of the tracks to the basement auditorium, used for seminars, in the main building.

"The tunnel will also be used for moving equipment from one side of the tracks to the other for testing in some of the plants away from the main facility," he said. "It will be the first ever built under N&W tracks for private purposes."

Construction of the tunnel was directed by Plant Engineer Jim Goodell, who had suggested the idea when design of the Plant 1 addition eliminated loading doors used in transporting supplies and experimental products between engineering and manufacturing areas. "In addition to providing direct access, rather than trucking these things down the street, around the corner, and over the tracks, we can eliminate the danger and inconvenience of pedestrian crossings," he told Stocker.

Following long negotiations with the Norfolk & Western Railroad, Goodell's plan was accepted, and Lorain Products agreed to what Stocker described as "paying N&W annual rent for a hole in the ground." The tunnel, eleven feet in diameter, was excavated and shored with carved quarter-inch ribbed steel plates while trains passed overhead without interruption. Grouted with concrete, it provided a corridor 10 feet wide, 8 feet high, and 250 feet long.

Lorain Products continued to rely on product innovations to maintain the growth of its sales to communications industries. Among its most important new products of the early 1970s were controlled ferroresonant battery chargers, and high frequency DC-to-DC converters. Prepackaged power platforms and power vans provided an economical and quick method for installing complete power systems at small- to medium-sized telephone exchanges. Each contained the rectifiers for the main battery, CEMF (counter electromotive force) cells, alarms and voltage controls for the DC power distribution system, (DC-to-DC) converters for auxiliary service such as carrier, repeater, and coin control, and the complete ringing, tone, and interrupter plant, all of which were designed and manufactured by the company.

A comprehensive program of engineering, furnishing, and installing Lorain equipment utilized the long experience of engineers to generate a new source of revenue, in addition to improving sales potential for several products. UPS sales, which represented 10 percent of all orders, were boosted by development of a solid-state transfer switch and other new features.

The domestic sales force, still headed by Chuck Ramaley, was divided into eight districts, covering all fifty states. Many of the field men were engineers, and all had either worked at the home office or attended thorough training programs there. Each had a backup person in Lorain to forward messages, provide current information, and contact customers directly when necessary. To stimulate inverter sales, the company set up an industrial sales group within the Sales Department and signed agreements with manufacturers' representatives who reached the industrial market over most of the United States. As a result, these sales doubled in one year.

President Stocker continued to look always to the future, maintaining the high ratio of research and development engineers for which he had been known through the years and orchestrating the enthusiasm for keeping in the forefront of technical experimentation. In areas of lesser personal interest, however, he smilingly confessed to a stubbornness that demanded proof as a requisite for change.

In that respect, he resisted efforts of Rob Stephenson and Martin Huge to have an outside audit as the company grew in size and scope during the late 1960s. "Why should I pay someone from the outside to do what you are doing very well?" he asked of Stephenson. "Because we are working in pesos and dollars and pounds and other foreign exchange currencies, and we have reached the size where we must have outside verification of our finances, and the IRS strongly suggests we do so," the corporate secretary-treasurer replied.

Still unable to obtain authorization, Stephenson waited until Stocker was on a trip with his family in 1970 to make the decision himself. Stocker returned to discover that an outside audit, ordered by Stephenson, had been made in his absence. "Why did you do such a thing?" Stocker demanded. "Because it is absolutely essential that we have an outside audit," Stephenson answered. "Well," Stocker said, "I guess I left an open ticket for you when I left."

Several weeks later, after weighing the relative merits and drawbacks of outside audits, Stocker took the time to thank Stephenson and admit he had been wrong—something he never hesitated to do. If further justification for Stephenson's decision was needed, it would come in the near future. Unless extraordinary circumstances can be proven, a federal law requires outside audits for at least three years before a large corporation can be sold.

THIRTEEN

AGREEMENT
TO MERGE

Frequent inquiries from companies interested in purchasing Lorain Products elicited little response from Paul Stocker before the 1970s. With 60 percent of its securities held by the immediate family and the remainder owned by intimate friends and colleagues, the company hardly was in danger of conglomerate raids that seemed to be gaining increasing popularity as a means of expansion. Friendly overtures, appreciated as acknowledgement of the firm's reputability, were rebuffed courteously but firmly, usually after minimal discourse.

Periods of ill health following his heart attack, however, prompted the president to ponder the possible benefits of selling the company. Steady growth in net sales and income made it an attractive property; recent offers confirmed that fact. The company had reached a level where continuing capitalization afforded by a larger organization should accelerate its growth. Establishing a substantial estate would assure the financial security of his family and provide a permanent base for his varied philantropic endeavors. Yet, he was equally concerned that all employees would benefit from the sale as well. That guarantee, he told Vice President Huge, would have to be cemented into any arrangement he would even consider.

In the spring of 1972, Huge, who was president of the Cleveland State University Alumni Association, was seated next to Hugh D. Luke, chairman and chief executive officer of the Cleveland-based Reliance Electric Company, at a university-sponsored dinner. Luke previously had said his company would be extremely interested in Lorain Products if Stocker ever decided to sell, so Huge mentioned that the time might be right to pursue the idea. Within twenty-four hours, Luke contacted Stocker to arrange a meeting.

Stocker insisted that the proceedings of the following sessions be kept confidential. If an agreement should be reached, he wanted assurance that there would be no sensationalism in the reports. More important, he was unyielding in seeking a promise of job security and continuing benefits for employees as requisites to effecting a merger.

Fortunately, Hugh Luke shared Stocker's business philosophy. Some colleagues observed that the personalities of the two men were such that they might have appeared to be brothers if it were not for the fact that Luke was about six-foot-six, compared to Stocker's five-foot-seven. Neither was greedy. Both had risen from humble beginnings to industrial prominence. They were modest but highly capable, and each respected the other's integrity. Midway into the negotiations, the two men dismissed lawyers on both sides, who had been haggling over technicalities, sending them off to another room to argue while the company leaders themselves put the agreement together.

Although he agonized over selling the company that had been so much a part of his life, Stocker made a firm decision when he was certain it would be in the best interests of his family and employees. That December a letter of intent was signed whereby Reliance Electric would acquire Lorain Products in an exchange of stock valued at $37 million dollars, pending approval by shareholders of both companies. Announcements to the media reported also Stocker's intention to retire and to be succeeded as president by Huge. The purchase was not expected to be consummated until summer, Stocker said, "because we have much detail work to complete."

At a meeting in May, the Lorain Products Board of Directors accepted an agreement and plan of reorganization whereby the company would become a wholly owned subsidiary of Reliance Electric Company. Shareholders voted the following month to confirm that decision. Terms of the merger specified that "each share of Lorain common outstanding stock . . . shall be converted into and become 25.8611 shares of Reliance common."

The merger became official on August 7, 1973, at which time Stocker also announced that he would continue in an advisory role until the end of the year, with Martin Huge serving as the newly formed subsidiary's president. A week later Huge addressed employees over the PA system:

Moving into the position of president of Lorain Products is certainly a challenge and an opportunity for which I am most grateful. At the outset I would like you all to know, however, that I do not consider myself as exactly stepping into the shoes of Mr. Stocker. The tremendous job he has done in building Lorain Products into the organization we have today commands a special kind of respect. The name Lorain Products Corporation is closely identified with the name of C. Paul Stocker, and the Lorain Products name today is recognized by customers, suppliers, and employees alike as meaning highest quality and unquestioned integrity in products, in services, and in personal relationships. This is the structure Mr. Stocker has built, and it now becomes not just my responsibility, but *our* responsibility as a team to continue to build on this structure while maintaining its essential qualities. In joining with Reliance Electric Company, we believe we are joining an organization which will enable us to carry on in the Stocker tradition.

Yesterday, our supervisors had an opportunity to meet Hugh Luke, the chairman of the board of Reliance, and learn from him how Lorain Products fits into the Reliance picture. His answers to the many questions that were asked give reassurance that our existing policies and employee benefits will be maintained. Even more important, his comments showed how the merger with Reliance can help us increase our rate of growth and provide greater opportunities for our people. The meeting with Mr. Luke was an inspiration for us and a demonstration of some of the reasons Mr. Stocker had agreed to merge Lorain Products with Reliance.

In the past, whenever the responsibility for operating the company has been in my hands, I have enjoyed excellent cooperation from our people. I have every reason to believe I will continue to receive this kind of cooperation, and with it, the outlook for the future of Lorain Products is bright.

If I were to tell you that nothing is going to change under the new setup I would not be completely honest. Not everything can be exactly the same as it has been, but I want to assure you that I am committed to maintain those policies and practices which have helped Lorain Products grow and which have made working here a satisfying experience.

First among these is fair treatment for each person as an individual and the opportunity for each person to be heard when the need arises. We have called this our open door policy. It has worked in the past and we want to keep it working. There have been times when some of you have had to wait longer than you should have for a chance to talk to me because I was involved in too many aspects of our company operations. This situation should be improved with the help of Donald Samson, who has been added to our organization as vice president of operations. Mr. Samson comes to us with a wealth of management experience, which should be very helpful to us in achieving our potential as a company. He will be overseeing our manufacturing, engineering, and marketing operations, and his door is definitely included in the open door policy, not only for problems and complaints, but also for suggestions for improving our operations. Rob Stephenson, Ben Norton, and Dick McMillan will continue to open their doors to you when you ask, and I hope the spirit of teamwork that has been a Lorain Products tradition will continue and grow. To have a winning team, we need the best efforts of everyone, and we expect to give recognition to contributions to that team effort.

About 80 percent of Lorain Products' $25 million annual revenues at the time of the merger was generated from sale of "standard catalog items." The balance consisted of products manufactured to order. Manufacturing affiliates of some large telephone companies made many of their own competing products, but Lorain Products nevertheless was a major supplier to the entire industry. It ranked at the top among suppliers to the independent telephone operating companies. Approximately 1,000 nonunion hourly employees and 250 salaried personnel made up the work forces at the Lorain complex and the Canadian and Mexican subsidiaries.

Reliance Electric had 16,700 employees, about 6,190 of whom were hourly rated and represented by labor unions. Eighty-five percent of the company's $400 million annual worldwide sales came from the manufacture of automation systems and equipment. Production of elevator systems and escalators accounted for the balance.

The automation systems and equipment Reliance developed, manufactured, and serviced were used to automate such industrial processes as batching, engineered drives, process control, and weight recording. An alphabetical listing of automation equipment manufactured by the company included analog and digital controls, converters, food machines, gearmotors, instruments, mechanical and electronic adjustable speed drives, mechanical power transmission equipment, motors, process control consoles, scales, soft-film wrapping machines, and solid-state regulators. This represented a broadening of its production lines over the past several years through acquisitions of Dodge Manufacturing, Toledo Scale, Custom Engineering, Applied Dy-

Paul and Beth Stocker and daughters Mary Ann (front), Nancy, and Jane (right).

Paul Stocker in office of F Street headquarters.

Beth Stocker and a grandson, 1966.

Lorain Products manufacturing complex just before sale to Reliance Electric in 1973.

Employee award is presented to Doris Coleman.

Fire threatens to destroy entire company complex on July 22, 1953.

Full line of products is ready for display at seminar for visiting engineers.

We hope everyone has a pleasant vacation this year. Remember -- July 9-23, 1961

Stocker enjoyed a surprise company-publication spoof of his celebrated attachment to a Volkswagen "bug" in 1961.

Paul and Beth Stocker.

President Stocker presides at a 1969 distribution of bonuses.

Portrait of Stocker in the company reception room.

At ground breaking ceremony for the Stocker
Engineering and Technology Center at Ohio
University in 1983, from left, Dolores and Fritz
Russ, Beth Stocker, and Eleanora and Richard Robe.

Main building of Lorain Products.

Martin Huge, seated, accepts an award on behalf of the company. Standing, from left, are Charles Leader of the Massachusetts Mutual Life Insurance Company, Rob Stephenson, and Ben Norton.

Ohio University's C. Paul and Beth K. Stocker Engineering & Technology Center.

namics, and Wrapping Machinery companies, each of which became a Reliance Electric division.

Another acquisition, Haughton Elevator, had moved it into the elevator-escalator industry, advancing in lockstep with the growing emphasis on high-rise buildings. Major improvements in the Haughton division were being achieved through advancement in technologies involving application of solid-state devices, integrated circuits, specialized computers, and electric motor design.

From corporate headquarters at 24701 Euclid Avenue in Cleveland, Reliance officers directed activities of manufacturing plants in Ohio, Michigan, Indiana, Wisconsin, Pennsylvania, Tennessee, and Georgia, through a network of groups and divisions. Subsidiaries and affiliates outside the United States were located in Australia, Belgium, Brazil, Canada, England, France, Germany, Japan, Mexico, New Zealand, Spain, Sweden, and Switzerland.

Acquisition of Lorain Products provided Reliance Electric's first entry into the telecommunications market, providing what Chairman Luke viewed as "opportunities for profit growth unmatched elsewhere in the company."

With the sale of Lorain Products, Stocker became one of nine outside directors serving on the Reliance Electric Company board, along with three corporate officers, Chairman Luke, President B. Charles Ames, and Vice President J. Allan MacLean.

In addition to the election of Martin Huge as president of the Lorain Products Division and Donald Samson as vice president, operations (with responsibility for marketing, engineering, and production), Robert Stephenson was named vice president, finance. Other veteran members of the management team at that time were: Richard McMillan, production superintendent; George Pohm, chief engineer; Alvin Pfaff, production coordinator; Frank Borer, service manager; Ben Norton, director of employee and community relations; James Goodell, plant engineer; William Christie, engineering administrator; and Charles Ramaley, sales manager.

Nearly all Lorain Products managers remained with the company after the merger. A notable exception, however, was Walter Krok. No chronicle of the company's history would be complete without the saga of this soft-spoken, imperturbable supervisor of the Rectifier Department who had used profits from youthful real estate ventures to help back Stocker's buyout of Fred Heavens in 1947.

Krok hadn't even remembered how many shares of stock he had purchased, because they didn't earn dividends and he never really expected any short-term gain. "I put the money in to help Mr. Stocker and because I had great faith in the situation," he said. "Usually people complain about what they buy, but everyone who bought our product praised it highly. So I thought it would be a good thing to be in. I didn't care how long it took, because I was sure Mr. Stocker would make it pay off."

When the merger agreement was finalized twenty-seven years later, Rob Stephenson called Krok on the interoffice telephone. "Stop by my office when you get a chance," the secretary-treasurer, suggested. "I have some figures I would like to show you."

When Krok arrived, Stephenson explained details of the merger agreement, then interpreted what they meant in terms of Krok's holdings. "The bottom line," he explained, "is that you are an instant multimillionaire."

Understandably startled by the news, Krok finally managed to reply, "You shouldn't have shown me those, Rob, because I'm going to resign." And that is what he did, after a friendly conversation with Stocker, who tried unsuccessfully to dissuade him from his decision.

"Even though this unbelievable thing happened, it wasn't just the money that led me to leave," Krok explained. "I knew from studying other situations that when one company buys another, it wants to make changes. I would do the same thing if I bought a company, so I wasn't being critical. But after all those years, it would have been impossible to have the same relationship I had with Mr. Stocker, so I decided to go out and look for other challenges."

The next summer Krok and his wife bought a camper and toured the West for the first time, accompanied by their daughter and a friend. In 1975 they moved to Florida. Instead of obtaining a large sum of money by selling his new Reliance stock, he kept it until events of the next few years increased its value tremendously, at which time it was converted to cash.

Well over a decade later, Mrs. Krok still had difficulty believing what had happened. The couple continued to enjoy a variety of new ventures, while living modestly and enjoying their family and long-time friends. It was only after strong persuasion that Krok even permitted the story— without exact figures—to be written. He was much more interested in reminiscing about the people and events he remembered from his thirty-three years at Lorain Products.

One episode during negotiations leading to the merger into Reliance Electric demonstrated that age had drained neither the devilment nor the competitive spirit from Paul Stocker. Through the years, Stocker had collected an assortment of specialized tools, which he kept in old wooden Velveeta Cheese boxes. When he suggested that these should be sold separately, Reliance representatives routinely agreed to the unusual request. They reacted differently, however, when Stocker later informed them, through Rob Stephenson, that the price would be $10,000. Although warned by Stephenson that Stocker would not bargain over the matter, the negotiators contacted the Lorain Products leader to voice their protest. "We've already discussed the matter," Stocker replied. Explaining that money had not been mentioned before, the group affirmed Reliance Electric's unwillingness to pay such a price for tools the company didn't need. "Well, then," Stocker said, "the merger is off." A few minutes later the discussion ended with agreement to pay the full $10,000 price.

A curious Rob Stephenson asked Stocker, "How could you possibly get away with that?" Stocker smiled impishly,

Stephenson recalled, and said, "Oh, you can squeeze things like that if you really want to."

"It was the old horse trader in action," Stephenson said. "We were talking about a multimillion-dollar deal, but he enjoyed squeezing out an extra $10,000 for something they didn't want."

FOURTEEN

TELECOMMUNICATION MILESTONES

Paul Stocker's "concession to retirement," said his wife, "was getting up at 5:30 instead of 5:00 A.M."

After retiring on December 31, 1973, Stocker served as a consultant for nearly two years. "Although he was in the office, he was very sensitive about not second-guessing anyone," Martin Huge said, "and he bent over backwards to avoid anything that would make me feel uncomfortable as president." Four hundred and sixty-six employees and friends attended a retirement dinner held in honor of the Stockers on January 5, 1974.

America's concern with an energy crisis, following a crude oil embargo imposed by eleven Arab states on nations deemed friendly to Israel, brought shortages of parts and materials needed for production in 1974. Yet, full employment was maintained throughout the year, and wage increases kept pace with inflation. In the first month of 1975, however, Reliance Electric released all Lorain Products Company employees over the age of sixty-five and those who were on part-time or probationary jobs. It was the first time in the company's history that employees were laid off because of a business slump. George E. Hindley, who joined Lorain Products as vice president, operations in November 1974 and later became general manager, explained the move as well as other "changes and actions" taken during subsequent months in a 1976 message to employees:

Most important to most of us, I believe, was what may appear to be abandonment of Lorain's historic policy of "job security no matter what." This is not the case. The economic problems the company reacted to were the worst we have ever seen. They could not be handled by temporarily operating at a loss to hold jobs. Lorain reacted correctly by changing the size of our operations to match the reality—which, in fact, is the only way to ensure true job security for the greatest number of employees. The change was made as fairly as we knew how, by seniority wherever possible and by job skills required, or by capability where these methods were proper.

When Lorain joined Reliance, it was the beginning of a longer term plan to create a Reliance Telecommunications Group consisting of Lorain plus additional companies. This Telecommunications Group will be similar in nature to Reliance's other groups of cohesive businesses such as Electric Group for motors and control, Mechanical Group for mechanical power transmission, and Toledo Scale for manufacturing and maintenance of scales. The Telecommunications Group is to be made up of acquisitions of other businesses selling other products to the telecom industry and of new products at Lorain, in addition to Power and Transmission. Martin Huge took on the major task of acquisition finding and evaluation. He has found several good candidate companies and Reliance has already negotiated to purchase one of them. A second is highly probable. Lorain is the cornerstone for this group.

Huge's assignment of heading expansion, acquisitions, and product development took him out of day-to-day management, although he retained the position of president. Both he and Hindley reported directly to Reliance President Ames, who described the move as "a step taken to put Reliance Electric in a better position to capitalize on the growth opportunities in the telecommunications field."

An engineering graduate of Lehigh University, Hindley had been with Reliance since 1955, advancing rapidly through management and engineering levels of the company. With the exception of Controller Richard Russell and Purchasing Director Robert Forshee (brought in from Reliance because of experience in the parent company's methods of financial controls and purchasing power), changes in major management positions involved long-time Lorain employees. Richard McMillan was placed in charge of overall manufacturing operations. Charles Scanlan managed material and production planning. Thomas McFadden became manager of printed circuit board operations and final electrical assembly. Al Wilson supervised a new Industrial Engineering Department, William Christie became supervisor of the large Engineering Department, and Ron Rebner was advanced to supervisor of the recently created Marketing Department. A "minibusiness" headed by William Chambers consisted of a separate group to engineer, produce, and sell transmission products.

The commercial UPS product line, supporting computers, was separated from other operations into a newly formed Power Systems Division. This was done to avoid putting high amounts of effort into UPS at the expense of the basic "bread-and-butter telephony power products," Hindley explained. Soon afterward, in mid-1977, the entire UPS line was acquired by Lorain Products employee Thomas O'Neill and two other investors who formed Lor-Tec Corporation to manufacture uninterruptible power systems in Elyria. (Lor-Tec merged with International Power Machines in 1989).

In February 1977, Martin Huge retired, after helping arrange for Reliance Electric Company's purchase of Reliable Electric Company, a Franklin Park, Illinois, producer of lightning protection equipment, cable termination points, and cable and wire splicing devices. With that acquisition, Lorain Products became part of a new Telecommunications Group, headed by Reliable President Robert J. Rodday. A third division was added to the group the following year when Reliance organized Lorain Telephone Electronics, Inc., at

Newnan, Georgia. The new plant, headed by General Manager Donald Bozeman, manufactured electronic equipment for use by the telephone industry. Manufacture of transmission product lines was phased out at Lorain during the next few months and moved to Georgia.

Plants 5 and 6 in Lorain meanwhile were sold to Wyatt Machine, Inc., a rapidly growing manufacturer of machines for the tool industry. (Manufacturing, service, and maintenance operations there were transferred to available space in other company plants.) Sale of the buildings prompted rumors that Lorain Products might leave the city. These were dispelled by General Manager Hindley, who told newspaper reporters, "Our parent company is pleased with the Lorain operation." He predicted steady growth for the sudsidiary, and activities of coming years proved him to be right, even though events were to follow a pattern neither he nor anyone else expected.

Exxon Corporation in 1978 was searching for an acquisition that could give it mass-production capabilities for an energy-saving "alternating-current synthesizer" its own engineers had been developing at research laboratories in Florham Park, New Jersey. The device was expected to combine power transistors with a microprocessor to raise the efficiency of electric motors. Its potential for sales, Exxon believed, was enormous. After examining several possibilities, the oil giant focused on Reliance Electric.

Following lengthy negotiations beginning in April 1979, Exxon, through its wholly owned subsidiary ENCO, Inc., made a tender offer of $72 a share for Reliance common, which was selling for $34 (a drop from $40 brought about by announcement of Reliance Electric's intention to purchase the Federal Pacific Electric Company). Exxon also offered $202.72 for each share of Series A preferred stock. When the offer ended on July 13, Exxon had received 95 percent of Reliance's common stock and 72 percent of its preferred stock. The total $1.17 billion offer was one of the largest cash bids ever made for an American company at that time.

The mammoth offering, however, went into limbo when the Federal Trade Commission attempted to block the merger on the grounds that it would eliminate potential competition between Reliance and Exxon, because the latter already had taken preliminary steps to commercialize the synthesizer. This obstacle was removed to the satisfaction of Reliance when U. S. District Judge John J. Pratt ruled that the two companies could merge but could not mix businesses that developed technology and manufactured energy-saving devices for electric motors. Exxon, not sharing Reliance's satisfaction with the ruling, considered rescinding the offer, but relented after the Cleveland firm said it would "take appropriate action" in the courts for the benefit of its shareholders. Judge Pratt also softened his order, enabling Exxon engineers to at least work with the Reliance group producing finished motors, even though they could not cooperate in developing the electric components.

Ironically, little more than a year after the merger became final on September 24, 1979 (official transfer did not take place until March 31, 1980), the synthesizer project was abandoned. Charles Ames, who had become chief executive officer of Reliance and had orchestrated the company's negotiations on the sale, told Exxon officials they had "made the right strategic decision, but for all the wrong reasons."

New ownership had little noticeable effect on the people of Lorain Products. When George Hindley was promoted to head of Reliance Electric's newly formed Components Group in Orlando, Florida, early in 1980, Walter M. Miller, who had been director of engineering at Lorain Products during the past four years, was promoted to general manager.

With the beginning of a new decade, Miller envisioned major changes in the telephone communications industry, brought about by FCC regulations and technological advancements. "Between 33 and 35 percent of our business today has been generated in just the last four years," he told *Lorain Journal* staff writer Bob Cotleur. "When a major customer asked if we could come up with a new power plant, we recognized it as a coming market, so we said we would give it a try. It took a company-wide effort, because it affected all parts of our operation."

"They were successful," Cotleur reported. "The new unit, a custom module called C-mod for short, provided a thousand watts of power in a package about two feet square. Connected to the main power source, it lets one bleed off six, eight, twelve, or twenty-four watts, or whatever, and become the heart of the company's PBX [private branch exchange]. That's the system that lets you hold one number and dial another, gives you a beep when you're talking and another caller is camped on waiting."

Before joining Lorain Products, Miller had been an Atlas Rocket booster control systems officer at Huntsville, Alabama, and a group leader for the worldwide space craft communications systems at NASA's Mission Control in Houston. Later he had worked with medical and chemical companies, designing and developing new product lines and systems.

Asked by Cotleur to comment on Paul Stocker, Miller said:

Now there was a man with vision. He launched this company when telephone companies were using reeds for ringers and were constantly annoyed when a reed wore out. Mr. Stocker invented the first solid-state ringer, and one of them still is hanging over the door in Plant 2. I think the real thing we've got at Lorain Products is the base built by Paul Stocker to serve the telephone industry. He could see the expansion coming— the real need for power in this area—and he developed something that helped significantly.

In 1980, the parent organization formed Reliance Communications Technology Company, encompassing Lorain Products; Lordel Manufacturing Company of Monrovia, California; LTE Transmission Products, Newnan, Georgia; Reliance Telecommunications Electronics Company, Bedford, Texas; and Reliable Electric Company, Franklin Park, Illinois. Telecommunications plants in Canada and Mexico and joint ventures in France and Japan were included also.

Popularly known as Reliance Comm/Tec, the new division, headquartered in Chicago, was headed by Robert Rodday, by then a corporate vice president.

John Morley, who succeeded Charles Ames as president and CEO of Reliance Electric in 1981, said formation of the division was "an evolutionary step in Reliance Electric's involvement with the telecommunications industry worldwide. Individually, the five companies making up the group are leaders in their product areas and collectively they enable us to provide telephone customers with products used from the central office to the subscribers' premises."

Lorain Products made the inside power equipment, Reliable the transformers and outside equipment, and LTE Transmission the voice frequency line treatment equipment, the president said. Lordel was a major supplier of electronic testing equipment, and Reliance Telecommunications was world leader in pair gain systems.

Reliance Electric's 1981 annual report speculated that the technical evolution from analog to digital transmission and switching would have long-term implications, adding, "This is especially true for products designed for the interoffice trunking and subscriber loop domains; several segments within these markets are receiving R&D attention, particularly fiber optics applications."

During the following two years, while overall Reliance sales and revenues declined markedly, the corporation's telecommunications group showed record profits. The difference in revenues could be traced easily by comparing the burgeoning telecommunications industry with key markets of other Reliance divisions, namely mining, energy, machine tools, and metals.

In 1983, the plant in Newnan, Georgia, became a remote facility of Lorain Products, rather than a separate member of the Reliance Communications Technology Company. Products built there were moved to R-TEC Systems in Texas, providing added capacity for the manufacture of Lorain Products power supplies for PBX telephone systems. (Four years later, however, the Newnan plant was closed, and the manufacturing of power supplies once again was consolidated at Lorain. Reasons given for the shutdown were technological changes that dramatically altered the products and the manufacturing resource needs, efficiencies gained in operations at the main center in Lorain, and the decision of a major customer to begin manufacturing the products itself.)

One of the most significant events in telephone history took place in early 1982, triggering economic reverberations with sufficient strength to modify the game plans of widespread business and industrial companies, including Lorain Products. After seven years of litigation, the U. S. Department of Justice succeeded in breaking up the world's largest corporation, American Telephone & Telegraph Company. The marathon antitrust case tried in District Judge Harold H. Greene's Washington courtroom had cost the government nearly $14 million and AT&T $360 million. It had produced more than a million pieces of paper, prompting a visiting judge, John J. Sirica, to quip, "I'm glad I only had Watergate."

In the negotiated settlement, AT&T agreed to relinquish twenty-two divisions of the Bell Telephone System with assets totalling $80 billion. AT&T could, however, retain its long-distance network, Western Electric manufacturing subsidiary, and Bell Laboratories, as well as be freed from a 1956 consent decree barring it from entering the computer business. Thus, a virtual monopoly was forced to give way to competition for long-distance customers, but AT&T actually could look toward long-term benefits by entering new communication arenas opened by deregulation.

Nearly ten thousand telephone people spent the following two years working out complex details of the divestiture under the watchful eye of Judge Greene. The dramatic change was confusing, not only to the public, but even to those working on the project and members of the regulatory commission. Meanwhile, large independents such as GTE,

Southern New England Telephone, and United Telecommunications stepped up plans to diversify into equipment manufacturing and other unregulated businesses, and IBM bought a large share of a company preparing to market equipment capable of switching large volumes of information beween telephones and computers. Battle lines were drawn among companies seeking long-distance subscribers.

January 1, 1984 became known as D (for divestiture) Day or One One Eighty-Four, when the official changeover took place. After the holiday, nearly a million employees returned to work at their regular jobs, but under new corporate structures. The former twenty-two Bell operating companies were split into seven independent regional corporations—Bell-South, NYNEX, Bell Atlantic, Ameritech, Pacific Telesis, US West, and Southwestern Bell—blanketing the nation. In addition to providing service through local operating companies, each regional corporation was permitted to sell, but not manufacture, telephone equipment.

As a manufacturer of telecommunications equipment, Lorain Products had to analyze possible new markets and new competitors seeking to supply those outlets. "Deregulation and the breakup of AT&T's Bell System set off powerful forces for change in our business world." General Manager Miller explained. "No longer would the status quo, no matter how good, be good enough. Change was inevitable. Companies that could adapt would survive, while companies that could not change would not survive. Lorain is a survivor."

Miller's prophecy proved correct. The regional Bell operating companies, soon referred to as R-BOC, worked individually with Lorain Products. The company in fact, found it benefited greatly from the good relationships Paul Stocker insisted on maintaining through the years, even though the Bell groups were required to purchase equipment from Western Electric. Now Lorain could sell to them directly. "It was a big opportunity and it paid off," a member of the management team said. "And as time went on, R-BOC groups became increasingly independent, so Lorain Products had all of these major corporations, as well as the independents as good direct customers."

———

Spurred by a year-long oil price collapse and an admitted lack of knowledge concerning the electrical equipment business, Exxon Corporation announced on December 11, 1986 that it was selling Reliance Electric Company. The purchaser was a group made up of John Morley and other Reliance officers who had arranged to finance a leveraged buyout through Citicorp Capital Investors and Prudential-Bache Securities. The price: $1.35 billion.

Under the new organization, Reliance Comm/Tec was incorporated in Delaware, becoming a separate business enterprise. Again, the ripple effect of changing ownership barely reached employees of Lorain Products, although pressure was felt by management to generate cash for interest on the parent company's large debt, incurred by financing the buyout.

A Comm/Tec booklet defined individual responsibilities of the company's major units:

> Lorain Products, founded in 1936 in Lorain, Ohio, specializes in designing and building central office power systems, inverters, converters, rectifiers, uninterruptible power systems, and power system monitors.
>
> The oldest unit, Reliable Electric/Utility Products, based in Franklin Park, Illinois, began manufacturing telecommunications hardware in 1909. Today, Reliable markets a wide range of products including connection, protection, distribution, and terminal equipment, as well as enclosures.
>
> R-TEC Systems is located in Bedford, Texas, and was formed in 1965, and it is an old timer in loop electronics, with more carrier patents than any other company in the business. R-TEC produces both analog and digital carrier systems, automatic loop-testing gear, and loop treatment products.

The newest member of the organization, Chicago-based Reliance Comm/Tec, was formed in 1987 to handle sales and marketing of T1 test and transmission products developed by the group's Advanced Development Laboratory in Richardson, Texas. The ADL also complements the individual engineering organization of each operating unit in the development of new telecom products.

Lorain Products sales fell in 1987, when a major customer decided to manufacture power products internally and new digital telephone switches requiring less power per line altered some instrumentation. The company rebounded, however, by introducing a new line of compact, decentralized power modules operating in the megahertz range, and by making changes in its sales and marketing functions.

When Walter Miller was named general manager of Reliance Electric's R-TEC systems plant at Bedford, Texas, in 1988, he was succeeded at Lorain by Hubert Owen, who had headed Comm/Tec international sales and marketing operations in Chicago. One year later, in June 1989, Owen returned to the Chicago headquarters of Comm/Tec Corporation, and Pete Paradissis became vice president and general manager of the Lorain Products Division.

Since serving as manager of research and development in the 1960s, Paradissis had risen to director of engineering at Lorain, then general manager of Reliance Comm/Tec Canada in St. Thomas, Ontario. He returned to the United States as a project manager at Texas R-TEC Systems, then moved back to Lorain in August 1988 to become director of sales and marketing. By that time, he held seven U. S. and Canadian patents and had written several technical papers presented at conferences and published in telecommunications industry magazines.

When she was told that Paradissis had become the new general manager, Beth Stocker expressed the assurance that, "Paul would have been proud and pleased to get such news." She said her husband always had been happy with accomplishments of the young engineer he had recruited so intensely at Ohio University, and had encouraged him to continue studying part-time toward a master's degree in business administration (which Paradissis received from Baldwin-Wallace College in 1984).

Indeed, the new head of Lorain Products acquired much of his business philosophy from the company's founder, particularly his belief in getting to know employees by visiting them regularly at their jobs.

On the wall of his new office, where he had been interviewed as a prospective employee twenty-eight years earlier, Paradissis hung a plaque he had received from employees of the Canadian plant he headed for two years. Under the bronze replica of a shoe were the words, "MBWA Award 1986-1988 presented to Pete Paradissis by Reliance Comm/Tec Canada."

MBWA, of course, stood for Management by Walking Around.

FIFTEEN

SERVING EDUCATION

Ohio University in the late 1960s and early 1970s experienced severe enrollment declines, attributed to a combination of student turmoil on American campuses, changes in state policies that led to both a growth in the number of competing public-supported universities and a surcharge for out-of-state students, and internal strife among groups struggling to protect individual departmental interests. Budgets became thin, and administrative changes frequent. Two years after Dr. Richard S. Mayer, a professor of chemical engineering, was named dean of the College of Engineering and Technology in 1971, he noted that in the flurry of transitions, the Board of Visitors "seems to have sputtered, stalled, and become well nigh extinct." To revitalize it, he asked Paul Stocker, who had been one of its most faithful members when the board was active, to serve as chairman.

Although he was in the process of selling his company to Reliance Electric Company, Stocker accepted chairmanship of the group, which Dean Mayer viewed as "providing services ranging from being a sounding board for some of our new ideas relating to the operation of the college, constructively criticizing the organization of curricula, listening to our financial problems, and being instrumental in helping find good adjunct professors, all the way to being financial angels for a student scholarship program."

In examining disciplines with high costs per student, however, some Ohio University administrators, led by Dr.

Taylor Culbert, executive vice president and dean of faculties, in 1973 proposed solving part of the monetary problems by phasing out the College of Engineering and dispersing its resources among other academic areas.

Dr. Reuben M. Olson, then a professor of civil engineering, later analyzed the predicament in his *History of the College of Engineering and Technology:*

The proposal was, in part at least, the result of several widely-held beliefs of the time. On one hand, were some who felt that the university should dedicate itself almost exclusively to the liberal arts, and to social and natural sciences. Others believed that the college was overstaffed and overfunded when compared with other colleges within the university, and, as a result, that those other colleges were subsidizing engineering. And finally, there was an erroneous belief that engineering students were isolated from the rest of the campus, and that they took only engineering courses. Actually, engineering majors took a minimum of forty-one percent of their course-work outside the college at that time.

Paul Stocker, who was beginning the last year of his second term on the Board of Trustees, as well as serving on the engineering Board of Visitors, was infuriated at such a suggestion. In a strong letter written shortly after his retirement from Lorain Products, he sought assurance from Ohio University President Claude Sowle (who had succeeded Vernon Alden in 1969) that budgetary revisions would not eliminate engineering. His concern extended also to other high-cost specialized academic areas that he considered vital to the healthy diversification of the university.

"I don't think Paul's letter made the total difference on whether or not the College would survive," said Dean Mayer, who understandably shared Stocker's displeasure, "but it was effective, and it provided a thrust that continued through the years. It was not his style to be visible and loud, so he followed up on the letter by talking quietly with other trustees and friends. And when Paul talked, people listened. I suspect that many influential persons were well aware of his feelings."

Admittedly, an overabundance of professional engineers had caused engineering enrollment to decline more sharply than that of the overall university. To address the resulting problem of staff imbalance, one of the university administration's strategies had been based on encouraging engineering and technology faculty to increase their contributions to general studies. With this policy in mind, Dr. Culbert agreed to the guarantee of survival, with the provision that some knowledge of engineering and technology would be made available to students in other academic disciplines.

At his final meeting with Ohio University's Board of Trustees in May 1974, Stocker was presented a Certificate of Appreciation for "exceptional membership" during the past fourteen years. The following month, he received the honorary degree Doctor of Engineering at the university's commencement:

> Presented to C. Paul Stocker. Dedicated engineer and master researcher, you invented and manufactured products that revolutionized the communications industry throughout the world. Your professional career has set an example not only for your fellow engineers, but also for all businessmen. Your outstanding accomplishments have benefited Ohio University in many ways.

Interestingly, the hood of honorary doctoral recognition was placed on Stocker's shoulders by Dr. Taylor Culbert.

———

Paul and Beth Stocker had been among the earliest members of the Trustees' Academy, the highest level of annual giving to Ohio University. Among the other gifts they already had given to their alma mater were endowed scholarships in engineering and other academic areas, financial contributions to the library, and special grants, the latest of which was an unrestricted $100,000 stock donation.

In January 1975 they added an $86,000 scholarship fund to benefit students in the College of Engineering and Technology and the College of Arts and Sciences. Annual dividends from the fund aided freshmen and sophomores majoring in engineering, mathematics, physics, chemistry, premedicine, and other related areas.

Later in the year, Stocker accepted a three-year appointment to the Ohio University Fund Board of Trustees. A nonprofit corporation, the fund was responsible for assets of $4.5 million, including endowments totaling $2.1 million. It also managed allocation of some $1 million in annual private gifts from alumni, friends, corporations, and foundations. All of these figures were to grow considerably in the years ahead.

On September 1, 1975 Dr. Charles J. Ping became the eighteenth president of Ohio University. A former professor and provost at Central Michigan University, the new president also was a regular summer lecturer at Harvard University's Institute for Educational Management. Believing that the Ohio University community had lost its confidence in the face of fiscal and enrollment crises as well as bad press resulting from the internal problems, Dr. Ping began the recovery process by restructuring the senior administration to emphasize the university's "academic mission" and improve its fiscal management. In-depth discussions were held with trustees, campus leaders, faculty, staff, students, and alumni leaders, to develop a long-range plan that would "enhance faculty life and compensation, recruit and retain quality students, and redesign curricula to insure the highest quality education and insure the value of undergraduate degrees."

At a convocation address, "The Search for Community," Dr. Ping, who earlier had described the university as "troubled, but rich in people, place, and history," identified six "relevant commitments" that would form the core of his plan for rejuvenation:

1. The commitment to the idea of a university and to being a residential college community.
2. The commitment to quality and to the making of judgments.
3. The commitment to intellectual community; to the interaction of knowledge.
4. The commitment to international community; to education for interdependence.
5. The commitment to lifelong learning; to the creation of a broad community of learners.
6. The commitment to educational justice; to being a just and socially responsive community.

Paul and Beth Stocker were among those greatly impressed with the university president's leadership and supportive of his ideas. At their invitation, Dr. Ping and the university's director of development, Jack G. Ellis, visited them several times to discuss proposals for additional financial support. The result was an anonymous gift of stock certificates, by far the largest contribution ever made to Ohio University. The gift established an endowed visiting professorship to be rotated among engineering departments, faculty enrichment funds, library support, and assistance for students with exceptional academic ability.

Seven annual scholarships also were provided for incoming students whose apparent potential for success was not reflected in their high school grade averages. Ellis, who later became a vice president of the University, described Stocker's reasoning behind that unusual request:

While we were making plans for various uses of the endowments, Paul said, "I want to set aside some monies that will go to ordinary students who need some help, if you can identify them as having good work ethics and the desire to succeed, even though they don't possess the greatest mental acuity you might prefer." He wanted us to locate these young people who are "willing by hard work to go forward with their academic careers," explaining "I want to help them, because that's the kind of person I was. With some of today's parameters for higher education, I don't think I would have qualified as a high school student coming to Ohio University. I think I would have been over-looked. My ambition in high school was to be the best auto mechanic that ever was."

Through his work on the University Fund board, Stocker was aware of a feasibility study that had been made for a major campaign and supportive of the idea that it should be shelved temporarily while internal university problems were being solved. When that was accomplished plans were resumed, with launching of the "1804 Campaign" set for the university's 175th anniversary in 1979.

"As we began building a base for the campaign, Paul and Beth Stocker provided funding to cover the cost of planning, developing materials, and the many other things needed to begin such an ambitious effort," President Ping said. "They also were among the most active participants, meeting with a group to discuss proposals on how the campaign could be conducted. As before, they insisted on receiving no publicity about their generosity."

Stocker served with two other distinguished alumni and former Board of Trustees colleagues, Edwin L. Kennedy and John W. Galbreath, in co-chairing a committee formulating further plans for the fund drive.

Having become a charter member of the Trustees of Lorain County Community College Foundation in 1974, Stocker also put his enthusiastic support behind that organization and soon became both a leader and a benefactor of its major projects. One in particular involved the foundation board's ambivalence on constructing a building devoted entirely to the arts and humanities. Discussions of such a project recurred time after time at board meetings over a period of nearly two years, always with strong endorsement from

Stocker, who considered it a much-needed facility for students and the community. Many complexities of state and district financing were studied, and figures indicated a need for approximately $1.5 million to be raised by the foundation. Various presentations followed on whether or not this support would be possible.

As in his business dealings, the Lorain Products president remained patient until he thought all avenues of debate had been exhausted. Then, in the quiet but forceful tone of voice that had come to identify his arrival at a positive determination, he said at a combined meeting of the foundation and college district boards, "It is time to quit talking and get going." As an initial incentive, he immediately pledged half a million dollars if fund raisers could match that amount. "That kicked us off," President Olson said. "He held so much respect, we knew we had to be successful and we were." Stocker made his contribution in the form of Reliance Electric common stock, which grew in value before the college converted it to cash.

Three years later, on November 29, 1977, Stocker took part in groundbreaking ceremonies for the $7.3 million building. Unfortunately, however, he did not live to see its completion in 1980, nor to learn that it would be named the Stocker Humanities and Fine Arts Center.

Although he had recovered fully from his 1969 heart attack and followed a disciplined regimen of exercise and proper diet, Paul Stocker began to lose his strength about three years after selling his company in 1973. Tests showed that he had contracted a rare form of lymphoma, a cancer of the lymph system that required a long series of blood transfusions at the Cleveland Clinic. The disease was kept in full remission for nearly five years; then his health deteriorated rapidly, until it was difficult for him to walk. The illness was particularly frustrating for a man who always had complete control of his life, but he never complained. Neither did Beth Stocker, who drew strength from her religion, her family, her friends, and the determination she always had shared with her husband.

In August 1978 all members of the Stocker family were together in Lorain when Paul became extremely ill and was taken to St. Joseph Hospital. He died on August 23. "I'm convinced that he managed to hang onto life until he could see all of us together once more," insisted Nancy Stocker Woodling.

To make certain employees of Lorain Products would be among the first to know of his death before reading about it in the newspaper, Beth Stocker asked her son-in-law, Ben Norton, the company's manager of employee relations, to announce it over the PA system. The next day, an editorial in the *Lorain Journal* expressed the feelings of thousands who had known Stocker:

> Honors were heaped on Paul Stocker before he died at 74. "Engineer of the Year" from industry and "Man of the Year" from his hometown of Lorain. Ohio University named Paul and his wife, Beth, "Alumni of the Year."
>
> But the real Paul Stocker left a legacy that few men—rich or poor, powerful or humble can match. He had the love and respect of his friends, family, his town, and the hundreds of men and women who worked with and for him at Lorain Products.
>
> For Paul Stocker proved that the American dream was genuine. With an associate, he started Lorain Products with little more than hope, his talent, and determination. He eventually established a multi-million-dollar firm with plants in Lorain, Canada, and Mexico, and, along the way, he built something just as valuable.
>
> Some called it a management style. To Paul, it was just his way of doing things. He created a closeness with his employees and they were intensely loyal to him. It sounds trite, but it was true: He considered them a part of his family.

But even that was only one dimension of Paul Stocker. He cared. He cared about his town. He was especially active on the Library Board, the Girl Scouts, the Chamber of Commerce, and every worthy civic improvement project that came along.

He was generous with gifts to programs that would uplift Lorain and Lorain County. But he laid down one condition: Nowhere was his name to be mentioned publicly as the donor.

The spirit of friendship, humanity, and community service that was such an integral part of Paul Stocker will continue to live and flourish wherever people cherish honor, integrity, fidelity, and service above self.

Friends crowded the First Congregational Church of Lorain for memorial services on August 25. Although not as active in the church as his wife, Stocker had been a member since moving to Lorain, and had served on its Board of Trustees and Finance Committee.

The "Alumni of the Year" award mentioned in the *Lorain Journal* editorial had been determined before Stocker's death. It was presented to Beth Stocker by Ohio University President Ping at a homecoming program that fall.

In his will, Stocker bequeathed nearly 200,000 shares of Reliance Electric stock valued at approximately $8 million dollars to Ohio University, specifying that it be used for three purposes: A $600,000 endowment was to finance a visiting faculty chair in the Department of Electrical Engineering; the remainder—about $7 million—was to be divided equally between support of equipment and advanced engineering research and a contribution to the university's 1804 Capital Gifts Fund campaign, scheduled to begin in the fall.

"This remarkable gift reflects the love Paul Stocker had for Ohio University and his belief in the future of the institution," President Ping said when announcing the bequest. "Private funding provides the margin of difference between good and excellent programs. This is a tremendous step toward realizing basic goals of the university's Education Plan for the next ten years."

Stocker's gift, in fact, more than doubled the size of Ohio University's endowment fund. Yet, its potential soon proved to be far greater than anticipated. While the transfer of stock was taking place, Exxon's enormous tender offering for Reliance securities was being held up in the District Court. When litigation was cleared by Judge Pratt's ruling that September, shares received by the university from Stocker's estate were among those sold at the $72 price. William L. Kennard, treasurer and controller of the university, delivered the certificates to the Cleveland Trust Company, where they were surrendered for more than $14 million. This was divided in accordance with the formula set forth in the will between the College of Engineering and Technology and the university's 1804 Fund, which provided support for other academic areas.

A Stocker Merit Scholarship Fund for Lorain County Community College students was established by contributions from the immediate family, friends, private gifts from Lorain Products employees, and contributions from the Reliance Electric Educational Trust Fund. The scholarships, which included tuition, fees, and books, were offered first to children of Lorain Products employees; but if they did not meet academic qualifications, the scholarships became available to other graduating seniors in the county.

"Paul Stocker left a legacy of widespread support in Lorain County, and Beth has carried it forward," said Robert Kirkpatrick, development officer at Lorain County Community College, who was involved in raising funds for the Stocker Humanities and Fine Arts Center there. The center provided one of Ohio's most outstanding educational facilities for students of art, dance, music, photography, communications, drama, and cinema, with a theater for significant college-community cultural events. Revolving turntable sections could transform the theater into three separate soundproof areas for lectures and fine arts productions. Within a few years it evolved as the state's number one children's theater, as well as the site of as many as four hundred annual performances.

———

Dr. John D. Kraus, professor of electrical engineering at Ohio State University, and Dr. Fred Evans, Tyree Professor of electrical engineering at the University of New South Wales, Australia, became the first of many internationally known engineers to hold the visiting chair endowed by the Stocker bequest. Dr. Carleton Sperati, a research fellow with the Washington Works of E. I. du Pont de Nemours & Company in Parkersburg, West Virginia was the first to occupy the chair funded by the previous Stocker endowment for rotation among the other degree-granting engineering departments. "Our faculty and students will gain immeasurably through firsthand contact with such distinguished scientists," Dean Mayer said, "and lasting benefits will continue after each of the holders of the Stocker Chair leaves the campus." By the end of the 1970s, Ohio University and its College of Engineering and Technology again were growing in numbers and strength. Engineering enrollment alone had nearly doubled in five years to 965 undergraduates and 116 graduate students. Having served the college during difficult years, but also during the enjoyable period of recovery, Dr. Mayer resigned as dean, returning to full-time teaching in the Department of Chemical Engineering.

His successor in August 1980, Dr. T. Richard Robe, was the first Ohio University alumnus to become engineering dean. A 1955 honors graduate in civil engineering, he also had received a master's degree in mechanical engineering and served on the faculty three and a half years before going to Stanford University, where he was a National Science Fellow while earning his Ph.D. degree. He joined the University of Kentucky faculty in 1965, and had been associate dean for academic affairs in the College of Engineering there before accepting the deanship of Ohio University. His teaching at Kentucky previously had been interrupted briefly when he was a post-graduate research fellow at the University of Edinburgh, Scotland, in 1973, and when he spent the 1970-71 academic year as a special assistant to the president of the University of Kentucky.

"The lure of the job at Ohio was the challenge and opportunity it offered," Robe said. "I'm convinced the opportunity exists to build research and graduate programs that can make the college one of the nation's top engineering schools. This potential was created by the bequest of Paul Stocker."

Allocations of interest income from the new endowment, in addition to the visiting professor's chair, supported increased computerization, research equipment, scholarships, fellowships, and faculty enrichment programs. As a less direct benefit, Robe counted on the endowment and flourishing enrollment to be "persuasive factors when consideration is given to the university's request (to the state legislature) for a new engineering complex." A proposal for the long-sought facility was included in a capital improvements bill before the legislature.

After another year of anticipation, plans for the new complex were put into motion when the state legislature in the spring of 1982 made an $11,700,000 appropriation for the project in Amended Substitute House Bill 552. With initial phases of the architectural work already completed, Dean Robe announced the advertising of bids. The first stage, as explained by Alan H. Geiger, university planner and director of construction, would be remodeling an existing building, Crook Hall, constructed as a West Green dormitory in 1965, to become the core of the complex. New construction would provide a five-story facility capable of bringing together all engineering and technology departments that had been spread among several campus buildings during the past four decades. A large rooftop deck would permit activities, primarily in electrical engineering and avionics, that required antennae. The deck would also accommodate equipment used by mechanical engineers in expanding solar research. "We are confident the laboratories, classrooms, and other divisions of the center will compare in quality with any engineering facility being built anywhere," Geiger said.

The proposed new complex was named officially by a resolution passed at the spring meeting of the university's board of trustees:

Whereas, the building currently named Crook Hall is being renovated and new construction added for the purpose of providing instructional and research space for the College of Engineering and Technology, and

Whereas, the Trustees wish to honor two people who brought distinction to themselves and Ohio University, and

Whereas, Ohio University is enjoying the benefits of the contributions of this husband and wife whose support one for another in university-related projects was truly unique, and

Whereas their contributions were evidenced in diverse ways, including membership in such bodies as the Ohio University Board of Trustees, the Ohio University Fund Board of Trustees, the Ohio University National Alumni Board of Directors, and the College of Engineering and Technology Board of Visitors, and

Whereas, the College of Engineering has recommended the naming of the building in recognition of the significant contributions of these distinguished alumni to the development and enhancement of the College's and University's academic programs,

Therefore, be it resolved that the building be named the C. Paul and Beth K. Stocker Engineering and Technology Center.

President Ping along with former presidents Baker and Alden joined Beth Stocker as special guests at a ceremonial ground breaking on June 21, 1983. Dr. Fritz J. Russ, president of Systems Research Laboratories in Dayton and a member of both the Ohio University Board of Trustees and the College of Engineering Board of Visitors, served as principal speaker, reminding the assembled group that "it was only because of people like Paul Stocker, who had visions of what might be done and then fulfilled those visions, that a facility such as this could be built." Russ and his wife, Dolores, also were major benefactors of the college, funding two major endowments for excellence in engineering instruction and research, and a scholarship program for undergraduates.

Motivated by plans to complete the building in 1985, the fiftieth anniversary year of the college, a committee headed by alumnus Samuel D. Greiner, an engineering consultant and member of the Board of Visitors, launched Project 85 to raise $4.5 million for equipment and academic support. Another Board of Visitors member, Cliff E. Baker, group vice president with Morrison-Kundsen Company in Boise, Idaho, was vice chairman. Money from the drive was to help the college "best utilize its planned new Stocker Center," Greiner said. Dean Robe assured the committee that "every dollar contributed to the campaign will be put to work where it can have the most effective impact."

The College of Engineering and Technology moved into its new home nearly on schedule in its anniversary year. The $11.7 million project, largest in the history of Ohio University, had three and a half acres of classroom, laboratory, and office space under one roof, and incorporated twenty-five miles of cable and wire for voice, data, and video transmission, all part of the university's computing and communications system. Other high-tech features of the building included a computer-aided design and manufacturing network linking dual-screen work stations on the second floor with milling machines in the basement. A minicomputer system on the second floor drove drafting terminals on the fourth floor. All classrooms, including a large lecture hall, were clustered around the center of the complex, making it easy for students to reach and change classes. Departmental office areas and laboratories fanned out into wings.

The C. Paul and Beth K. Stocker Engineering and Technology Center was formally dedicated on April 10, 1986, described by Dean Robe as "a special day in the life of the college." In opening the program, the dean introduced three generations of the Stocker family, some of whom had traveled great distances to be at the dedication. Daughter Jane Norton, her husband, Ben, and their children accompanied Mrs. Stocker from Lorain. Daughter Nancy Woodling, husband Reese, and children, and daughter Mary Ann Dobras, husband Darryl, and children arrived from their homes in Tucson, Arizona. Doyle Stocker came from Seminole, Florida. Several former associates at Lorain Products and long-time friends also attended, as did top administrators and trustees of the university, to tour the facilities, join a capacity crowd at the featured program in the lecture hall (an overflow group watched it on closed-circuit television in another room), and take part in a dedication dinner.

The day-long program was capped by the dedication dinner address by William G. Simeral, executive vice president of du Pont, who told guests:

> Stocker Center represents an enhanced opportunity for this university to respond to the main challenges confronting technological institutions in our time: the challenge to innovate and the challenge to manage our technological resources effectively. While basic research in the sciences can claim as its legitimate goal the creation of new knowledge, the engineer has the additional responsibility of using new knowledge to create things that will make your lives better and our work more efficient.

Samuel Greiner reported that the Project 85 campaign had reached 98.6 percent of its $4.5 million goal through contributions from alumni, faculty, friends, foundations, and corporations. By the end of the year, it exceeded the goal.

By the beginning of 1988, all six degree-granting departments within the College of Engineering and Technology— Civil, Chemical, Mechanical, Electrical and Computer, Industrial and Systems Engineering, and Industrial Technology—reported growths in enrollments and programs.

That spring, the Department of Aviation added a bachelor's program in airway science, in response to Federal Aviation Administration projections that airline flights would more than double by the year 2000, requiring a 60 percent increase in the number of pilots and other professionals in the aviation industry. The department previously had offered a two-year associate degree in aviation technology, although it was not unusual for students completing that program to progress into engineering or other academic fields to work toward bachelor's degrees.

Dean Robe soon announced a five-year plan for the college, extending into 1993:

The plan builds on goals and achievements of the past five years, which provide an excellent set of initial conditions for the next five-year period. Our goals of 1982-87, including completion of the Stocker Center engineering complex and accompanying upgrading of facilities, academics, and research, have been largely met. Our new plans represent an update, with the basic mission of the college remaining unchanged. That mission is to attract and educate talented engineering students, to contribute to advancement of the profession and the public welfare, and to help develop practicing professionals by providing quality continuing education.

The five-year plan specified objectives and "action steps" for each area of engineering and technology. Among more than forty new goals were those focusing on student recruitment, scholarships, internships, student co-op opportunities, developing additional doctoral level studies, increasing the level of sponsored research, and supporting various instructional and research programs with direct applications to serving society.

The plan had been reviewed and endorsed by the College Board of Visitors, which included Russ; Greiner; J. David Carr, president of Pittsburgh-based Carr Consultants International; James M. Abraham, Columbus engineering consultant and retired assistant adjutant general for the Army, State of Ohio (with the rank of brigadier general); Walter D. Callahan, vice president and general manager of Cooper Industries' Apex Division in Dayton; Cruse W. Moss, chairman of the Flxible Corporation of Delaware, Ohio, and General Automotive Corporation of Ann Arbor, Michigan; and Robert H. Page, Forsyth professor and former dean of engineering at Texas A&M University. Dr. Page at that time also was serving as president of the American Society of Engineering Education.

The College of Engineering and Technology entered the 1990s with an enrollment of 1,555, representing a 44 percent increase from the year it received the endowment from Paul Stocker's estate. Sixteen Stocker visiting professors had brought special expertise to various curricula from responsible research positions in government, industry, and international universities. Ninety-four research projects were being carried out by faculty-student teams, many of them on specific assignments from NASA, the Federal Aviation Administration, state and national transportation departments, the U.S. Environmental Protection Agency, individual corporations, and various institutes seeking new knowledge on topics of critical public concern. Five special research centers attracted some $3 million annually in external funding. They included an internationally known Avionics Engineering Research Center and the more recently organized Center for Geotechnical and Groundwater Research, Ohio Coal Research Center, Center for Stirling Technology Research, and Center for Automatic Identification Education and Research. Each operated on an interdisciplinary basis, working across departmental and college lines so participating students could gain integrated knowledge from various areas. Dean Robe expressed the university's debt to the Stockers:

> Although support is mounting each year from many sources, including the university's own foundation, there is no question that the momentum, as well as a large percentage of continuing funding, relates directly

to the bequest by Paul Stocker and subsequent contributions from Beth Stocker. In my opinion, it is absolutely amazing how the loyalty and generosity of one couple triggered a movement that keeps expanding through the years, motivating others to join the cause, and creating opportunities for an ever-growing number of people. Paul Stocker did it with his company, and both Stockers have done it through Ohio University, Lorain County Community College, and many civic organizations. The number of individual persons who have benefited and will continue to benefit from what they have done is staggering.

In reflecting on early years of his administration, President Ping remembered vividly when Paul Stocker asked, "If you could describe one thing that would be critical to the good health of the College of Engineering and Technology in the decade ahead, what would it be?" With the college facing a fiscal crisis at that time, the president had replied, "I think the college will suffer largely by our inability to fund new instrumentation and research activity. I think we can support people already on the scene, and we must allocate essential dollars for the continued enhancement of equipment in order to meet those obligations to people. It is appropriate for that to be our first priority, but it is done at the expense of the good health of programs dependent upon instrumentation and research." After further discussion, Beth Stocker added, "I think it is very important that we not restrict whatever we do in ways that will make it difficult for the university to respond to change," Ping recalled.

"I had no idea what amount we were talking about, but I realized it was a major gift," the president said. "There was a clear intent that it must be done quietly, modestly. That, of course, was the way they approached both the earlier endowments and the bequest, and it is the way Beth Stocker has continued to help."

President Ping often referred to a segment of the bequest that he considered an example of exceptional insight and selflessness:

. . . to create with the greater part of my estate the gift of educational opportunity for the young of present and future generations, as we have had the enjoyment of the privileges and rewards of our educational opportunities during our lifetime.

"I think the trust of Paul and Beth Stocker opened the future of the College of Engineering and Technology and the university with their remarkable gifts," President Ping said. "Things have happened that would have given him great delight."

For several years before his death, Paul Stocker had discussed with his wife the possibility of establishing a foundation serving educational and cultural needs of the communities where members of their family lived. To carry that wish forward, Beth Stocker created the Stocker Foundation, incorporated as a nonprofit organization on November 14, 1979. Supported by money from her husband's estate, her own continuing contributions, and the appreciative value of the base endowment, the foundation grew from providing one grant in its inaugural year to sixty-four grants totaling well over half a million dollars a decade later. Although Beth Stocker served as president of the foundation, her daughter Jane (Norton) assumed operational responsibilities as executive director. The other two daughters, Nancy Woodling and Mary Ann Dobras, were on the board of directors, as was the oldest granddaughter, Anne Woodling, who represented the family's third generation.

Charitable grants to organizations benefiting residents of Lorain County and southern Arizona—about 98 percent of the total—cover a wide spectrum of medical, scientific, educational, day care, arts, and social services, with emphasis on youth-oriented projects. Whereas many private foundations are extensions of the donors' personal charitable giving patterns, the Stocker Foundation reflects a minimum of such special interests, one being that priorities are given to programs encouraging participants to help themselves, rather than simply accept handouts.

The foundation's structure wisely was made flexible by Mrs. Stocker so that focus can be changed with social evolution, thus avoiding narrow restrictions often locking foundations into channels that can be altered only by legal action.

"The needs of the world change dramatically, as does the makeup of society," Jane Norton explained. "Our objective is to change with them, and I feel certain this will continue. We intend to cover a broad range of programs that meet specific IRS regulations of being nonprofit and designed in the best interests of the public."

SIXTEEN

VINTAGE STOCKER

Paul Stocker was in awe of life and what it offered. Men and women with whom he worked spoke often of the inspiration they drew from his unique observations on the "wonderment of America."

On a trip with Sales Manager Charles Ramaley, who also had a rural background, Stocker glanced at a field they were passing and asked, "Chuck, when you were a young farm boy, did you ever think a person could get paid for doing anything except hoeing corn?"

"Now that you mention it, I don't believe I did," Ramaley replied.

"I'll bet it didn't seem possible then that someone would pay you later just for talking," said Stocker.

Reminiscing on the incident, Ramaley admitted he had "never analyzed sales in quite that light," but the comparison made him "forever pause and smile whenever I got to thinking I was working too hard."

Stocker never measured success in terms of finances or status—in fact, he never paid himself a high salary—but rather in how well one could help others set goals and work to achieve them. He was flabbergasted by society's deference to celebrity, power, and wealth, considering it demeaning and certainly illogical. And he was equally amazed at the insecurity he recognized in high-ranking executives who apparently felt entrapped in the pecking orders of many corporations. Despite their responsible positions, he believed they lacked the confidence to make decisions. That, in his opinion, was a serious industrial flaw. Loyalty too often flowed only upward through executive ranks. To Stocker, it had to be reciprocal.

"He treated people inside and outside his company in a way that caused them to enjoy what they were doing," said contractor Robert Woodward. "They knew good work was appreciated. What better enjoyment can you have than that? And he treated everyone the same. It didn't matter to him whether it was a laborer working for me, one of his own employees, a top client, or a visiting dignitary. In talking to him, there was absolutely no feeling that one person was more important than another. It was amazing."

Stocker bowled on the company team. He appeared at homes of employees on weekends to visit members of their families who were ill. In walking through the plant, he addressed each employee by his or her first name, with the lone exception of secretary Joyce St. Aubin, who joined the company immediately after graduating from Lorain High School; for reasons never explained by the president, he always called her "kid." (A colleague speculated that the reason probably stemmed from Miss St. Aubin's mother, Vera, working there since 1955, and her uncle being Walter Krok.) An Ohio University president noted that whenever someone at a reception for trustees asked Stocker what business he was in, the answer was, "I work at Lorain Products in Lorain, Ohio." Marie White, administrative assistant to five Ohio University presidents, always enjoyed greeting the Stockers when they visited the campus. "He was modest and unassuming, and she was a gracious lady," Mrs. White said. "They made a wonderful team."

Frank Borer, veteran service manager for Lorain Products, said, "Stocker's intelligence always came through, but he was a very humble man. And you know, people liked that combination. Customers appreciated it. And so did all of us at the company. It was just ingrained in him. He didn't have to act modest; he *was* modest. On one sales trip, the two of us were walking down a street in New York City and he stopped to get us each an apple, then he pulled out that sharp knife of his and cut off slices, eating them as we walked. Things like that made you always feel at ease with your president, but it wasn't playacting. That's just the way he was."

When company photographer Al Pelton offered to repair Stocker's malfunctioning camera one evening after work, the president delivered the camera to Pelton's house. "While I made the repairs, he stood there almost with his chin on my shoulder watching me and asking me questions. He always wanted to know about anything like that, and he seemed to admire what others could do. You felt totally relaxed around him."

Martin Huge remembered, "Paul seemed surprised that I considered it unusual for him to drive the Bell Telephone System president from the airport to our plant in his Volkswagen Bug."

Even the company's promotional philosophy reflected a rejection of affectation. "We didn't use a lot of flash when he headed the company," said Ray Young, who became head of advertising after Stocker retired. "All we did was show what we had and what it would do for a customer. Advertising was done on an as-needed basis, but we could get away with it then, because we didn't have the widespread competition that came later when the breakup of AT&T produced a whole gaggle of new markets to reach in a hurry."

What would have appeared as eccentricities in other personalities seemed quite credible when ascribed to the Lorain Products president. No one was able to explain this paradox. It simply was vintage Stocker.

"He carried that little pocket knife with him every day, and used a surgical sharpening instrument to keep it perfectly honed at all times," Al Pfaff recalled. "One morning when I met him in his office just after he arrived, he reached in his pocket and noticed that the knife was missing. With a brief apology, he put his hat and coat back on and went home to get it. For some strange reason, that seemed plausible to me. If it had been anyone else, I probably would have stood there scratching my head."

Stocker's tool kit, about half the size of an attaché case, was considered equally indispensable. He never made a trip without it. Justifying such an "idiosyncrasy" never would have occurred to Stocker, but if it had, he could have received endorsement from an international audience. In 1964, Paul and Beth became the only Americans in a British tour group (made up primarily of Europeans, New Zealanders, Australians, and Canadians) traveling by bus from India through the Middle East, Balkan States, and Middle Europe. During the three-month excursion, the group camped out nearly every night, staying at hotels only in major cities. Midway into the 10,000-mile trip, the bus began to develop a variety of mechanical problems, which would have reached disastrous proportions were it not for Paul Stocker, his tool kit, and other intrepid passengers. With no parts available in most areas along the way, Stocker spent many hours of his vacation under the bus, fashioning makeshift repairs that kept the vehicle mobile. "We made lifelong friends on that trip," said Beth Stocker, who still received letters from some of them twenty-five years later.

During frequent trips to Mexico, a favorite touring area for the family, Stocker found regular uses for his tools, particularly in small hotels. "I've fixed toilets all over Mexico," he told a friend.

———

Travel to the Stockers, in addition to being enjoyable, helped build close family relationships and expand the children's educational experiences. Those were considered fundamental elements of life's fulfillment by both parents.

During most of the 1940s, family travel was limited to brief excursions in Ohio and Pennsylvania. The only "vacations" the parents took alone were annual three-day trips to the Independent Telephone Association conventions in Chicago. "They would come home with presents and souvenirs from exhibitors' display booths and tell us wonderful things about Chicago," Nancy said. "I grew up assuming that it must be the most wonderful of all places."

More extensive summer itineraries developed late in that

decade, when the youngest daughter, Mary Ann, reached school age. "We explored the United States thoroughly, and made automobile trips to Canada and Mexico, stopping every time Dad spotted a scene he wanted to photograph— which was quite often," Mary Ann said. "Also, we stopped frequently to tour factories. Dad was intrigued by them, and would get permission for all of us to look them over. He was just fascinated by how things worked, so we went through all kinds of plants. I especially remember touring an alfalfa refinery with a stifling smell; we saw every piece of machinery and came away, as usual, with small samples of the product."

Over the years, the five Stockers visited every state except Alaska and Hawaii, driving by or walking through each capitol. In every area, Stocker's insatiable curiosity about different lifestyles was evident in what and whom he wanted to see. "I interpret his travel as one way of satisfying that intense curiosity," Nancy observed. "Of course, it was a great benefit to us too. We all enjoyed it, and continued to do so when we had our own families."

Beth Stocker served as navigator, using the AAA Tour Book as a guide. "That was her Bible," a daughter said. "She would read the historical information and points of interest to us, as well as refer to it for selection of restaurants and places to stay." Three skirts were kept folded on the back window ledge of the car so they could be put on over the girls' shorts when they went into a restaurant. Usually, their mother also took time to rebraid their hair before the evening meal.

The family's first venture beyond U. S. boundaries was a trip to Mexico, memorable in many respects, including an incident recalled in detail by Nancy, who was just ready to enter high school at the time:

> We were in Toluca market one day and even though dad was careful, a man jostled him while another picked his pocket. Realizing immediately what had happened, dad did not attempt to conceal his anger this

time, as he saw them getting away. So we all went to the police station, where he insisted that something be done, explaining that he could describe the men who stole his wallet. The police didn't seem overly concerned, however, so we headed for the American Embassy. Dad was worried about our tourist visas, and Mary Ann was afraid we would miss the bullfight, since the tickets also were in the wallet. Of course, we never saw the wallet again, but we did get new visas and more tickets for the bullfight. First, however, we marched directly to a leather shop, where dad had a very elaborate money belt crafted for him. He wore it conscientiously thereafter under his clothes.

On one trip, Stocker's elderly mother joined the family on a tour of several southern states. Still meticulous in keeping records, Cinderella Stocker, looking prim in her best dresses, hose, and heels, jotted information in a small notebook as they drove. "Grandma recorded the name of every city, town, and hamlet that we went through from Ohio to southern Florida and back," Mary Ann said.

In 1955 the family spent most of the summer touring Europe. One highlight of that trip was visiting Beth Stocker's brother, Walter Kilpatrick, his wife, Irene, and their daughter, Doris, who were living in southern Germany. Kilpatrick, who had graduated from the University of Pittsburgh and studied in England and Switzerland in the 1930s, spent nearly all his career in Europe, beginning with the War Prisoners Aid Program of the Geneva Convention during World War II, and later extending into refugee operations with Church World Service and World's YMCA. Irene died while they lived in Germany. (In the 1980s, several years after retirement, Kilpatrick and his second wife, Anita, moved to Prescott, Arizona. Doris married Firdauf Siddik, whom she met while attending The International School in Switzerland; they moved to his native country of Indonesia, where he established his own business, and had one son, Rick.)

All three Stocker daughters and their mother were active in Girl Scouts. Beth served in many volunteer roles leading to president of the Girl Scout Council. She accompanied troops to a national conference and helped scout leaders prepare for campouts and special events. When several local councils were to be consolidated into a larger northeastern Ohio organization, she chaired the task force that worked out the complicated arrangement. Her husband was supportive of her scout work, and when plans were made to buy land and build a residential camp, he accepted an appointment as chairman of the fund campaign. The combined leadership of the Stockers in successfully raising money throughout that part of the state led to naming the dining hall in their honor.

Despite being firm in disciplining his children, Paul Stocker always complimented them on things they accomplished—or tried to accomplish—to the extent that his meaning could be misinterpreted in young minds. Even when their cooking efforts brought results they knew stretched the limits of palatability, father's compliment was forthcoming, causing them to think he didn't know the difference between good and bad food. Determined to win a baking contest sponsored by Ohio Edison for junior and senior high school students, Nancy and Jane each spent several evenings working to produce a sponge cake according to exact specifications. At their request, Stocker dutifully tasted each sample, always offering a laudatory opinion, which remained unqualified when they failed to win the top prize. He did, however, confidentially express to his wife the hope that she "never make a sponge cake."

All members of the family looked forward to the annual "homecoming" when descendants of Closman and Cinderella Stocker gathered for Thanksgiving dinner at the farm in Tuscarawas County. Paul's brother Glenn had returned there in the Depression, after working several years for Procter & Gamble in Mississippi. Living with his family in a smaller house near the family home occupied by his parents, Glenn joined his father in building the dairy business into a successful enterprise.

With the burden of responsibility shifted from father to son in the 1940s, Glenn, his wife, Kathryn, and their two children, Sue and Sigel, traded homes with Closman and Cinderella. Twenty years later, Glenn and Kathryn built a hilltop house on the farm property, and their son moved into the original home after graduating from Ohio State University. None of those changes nor the growth in families disrupted the Thanksgiving get-together, although the site did shift to the new house on the hill after 1962. Kathryn Stocker died in 1974.

Doyle Stocker and his wife, Helen, also joined the group each Thanksgiving. Although he worked at various times for state and county departments and owned a hardware store (which brother Paul claimed to have the best inventory in Ohio), Doyle was best known as the tough law-and-order mayor of New Philadelphia in 1958-59. He and his wife had lost their only son in infancy. (After Helen died, Doyle married his second wife, Doris, in 1981, and later moved to Seminole, Florida).

In addition to farming, Glenn Stocker served in the unusual dual capacities of teacher and custodian at Claymont High School in Dennison for several years before retiring to a scaled-down farming schedule. His son, who obtained a doctoral degree and moved from the farm to become a laboratory researcher in Wooster, Ohio, and his wife, Mabel, had four sons—Eric, Kurt, Karl, and Jon—and a daughter, Amy Carol. Sue Stocker married Dr. John E. Romig, an optometrist with offices in Uhrichsville; they had two daughters, Stephanie and Melissa.

In 1985 Glenn Stocker died of injuries suffered when a tree fell on his head while he was operating a bulldozer to build the dam for a farm pond. After that, the Thanksgiving reunion was held at the Romig home in Dennison.

———

Living on the lakefront of Lorain, the Stocker daughters were good swimmers. Their father had enjoyed the sport as a youth, but an ear infection forced him to limit his time in the water. Yet, he frequently drove his boat to pull the girls and their friends on water skis. He seemed to get more enjoyment, however, working with Luther Marquart, a skilled mainte-nance specialist at Lorain Products (and also the father of three girls), in designing and building what they referred to as a "marine railway" that lifted the boat from the water, then transported it to a land-based dock. A long-time friend and neighbor, Wayne Conn, remembered that Stocker also "was always devising schemes to prevent erosion of the water-front." One of the most elaborate projects was a series of criss-crossed jetties that diffused the impact of incoming waves.

Always the perfectionist, Stocker was not satisfied with requirements for obtaining a driver's license. Consequently as each daughter reached the age of sixteen, she was required to pass her father's driving test before being permitted to take the official examination of the Ohio Department of Trans-portation. Mary Ann provided a vivid explanation:

> There weren't any big hills and curves in Lorain, so dad would take us to Mill Hollow, a park outside Ver-milion, which had a hairpin turn on a hill. Having taught us to stick-shift, he would instruct us to start and stop, upshift and downshift on that turn. Although I was fully capable of passing the regular state test, I failed dad's version twice, because of stalling the car. Without showing any impatience, he simply told me we would return the following weekend for another try. He knew I could pass the state test, but he said we would encounter "unusual situations you should know how to handle before they are emergencies." I was furious at the time, but after I had teenage daughters of my own, I saw some wisdom in it.

Participating in a variety of Lorain High School activities, each daughter sang in the choir, well known in the area for its outstanding presentations of operettas and concerts.

Paul and Beth Stocker celebrated their twenty-fifth anni-versary in 1955 by taking their daughters on an extended trip through Europe before Nancy entered Miami University at

Oxford, Ohio, in the fall, establishing a precedent that would be followed by her sisters.

At the end of her sophomore year, Nancy, who was preparing for a teaching career, married Reese Woodling, a geology major who had transferred from Western Reserve University in Cleveland. The couple had met three years earlier when Reese accompanied his father, a Cleveland patent attorney, on a trip to deliver some materials to his client and friend, Paul Stocker.

In the first year of their marriage, Nancy and Reese won fifty dollars in an oil company contest and decided to spend it on a western camping trip. A coin-flip decision favored Nancy's choice of Arizona over Reese's preference for Colorado, but the experience proved to be so enjoyable the difference of opinion quickly dissolved. They agreed, in fact, on moving to Arizona after graduation. Two years later, they began their careers in Flagstaff. Soon afterward, they moved to Tucson so that Nancy could earn a master's degree in education at the University of Arizona. Reese became a cattle rancher when they decided to remain in that city.

Jane followed her sister to Miami, where she majored in dietetics. Following graduation, she spent a year at the University of Minnesota Hospitals to become a registered dietitian. With subsequent job offers in central Colorado and northern Ohio, both of which locations were highly appealing, she chose the latter, accepting the position of dietitian at Elyria Memorial Hospital. The decision admittedly was influenced by having frequently dated Ben Norton, a young employee at the Lorain plant of U. S. Steel, whom she had known since childhood. After their marriage in 1964, Jane continued to work at the hospital until it interfered with raising her family. Later she served as a part-time teacher of nutrition at Lorain County Community College. Ben left U. S. Steel in 1965 to organize the Lorain Products Personnel Department, and later earned a master's degree from Case Western Reserve University.

Mary Ann attended Miami University for two years, then transferred to Ohio State University, where she received a degree in nursing. Before graduation, she married Darryl Dobras, an OSU business major whom she had known since they were in the fifth grade of a Lorain elementary school. After graduation, Mary Ann worked at University Hospital in Columbus while Darryl served a brief military tour of duty before they too headed for the University of Arizona, where he obtained a degree in architecture. Later, they moved to Houston while Darryl studied for a master's degree through a scholarship at Rice University. Then they returned to Tucson, where he became an architect and land developer.

Jane and Ben Norton had three sons: Ben, Bradley, and Brent. Mary Ann and Darryl Dobras had three daughters; Dawn and twins Amy and Wendy. Nancy and Reese Woodling had a daughter, Anne, and a son, David. As a dedicated engineer, Paul Stocker said he appreciated the perfect balance of grandchildren.

When Anne Woodling was four years old, she began another Stocker tradition by spending two summer weeks with her grandparents in Lorain. Three years later, when David reached that age, he joined his sister for the annual visit, which always proved to be an adventure.

Each summer, David worked with his grandfather on a creative craft project. Once, when both were puzzled about the solution to a mechanical problem, Stocker suggested that they sit down for a while. As they did, the grandfather got some walnuts from a drawer, pulled out a nutcracker, and they sat eating nuts for several minutes. Finally, he said, "David, I've got it." Thereupon they went back to work and finished the project. Many years later, David realized the respite had been "thinking time," when his grandfather "shifted gears" to let the creative juices flow at a relaxed pace. The grandson adopted the idea himself when, not surprisingly, he too became an engineer.

David recalled also that when he was ten years old, his grandfather taught him algebra. "Grandpa would sit down for about half an hour each day during my summer visit and show me how to do algebra," he said. "I was thrilled, because I thought only big kids could learn that."

Similarly, Brent Norton remembered his grandfather teaching his brothers and him how to operate a jigsaw, "under careful supervision, of course," at early ages. "Grandpa also showed us how to make paper airplanes that would go farther and faster than the usual kind made by everyone else, and when he used his knife to make a bow and arrow out of some green branches and a piece of twine, I felt just like an Indian in the forest."

During a walk with Brent along the beach, Stocker spotted a piece of driftwood that reminded him of a whale. Taking it back to his basement workshop, he cut out a mouth and an eye, then mounted it on another piece of driftwood for his grandson. When he was a student at Ohio Wesleyan in 1989, Brent still prized that reminder of early private outings with his grandfather.

When several of the grandchildren were together in Lorain, Stocker entertained them by linking tricycles and wagons into a train. Younger children rode in the wagons, while the older ones provided the train's tricycle power. Occasionally grandpa hunched up his knees and crammed himself onto the lead tricycle. He also revived the idea of building a "shock machine," entertaining the children as he had his classmates at Dennison many years before and receiving the same enthusiastic response.

On their forty-fifth wedding anniversary, Paul and Beth joined the entire family at a dude ranch in Montana. During that week, Stocker rode a horse every day. A year later, the effects of lymphoma began to take their heavy toll.

Many who knew Paul Stocker recognized an affinity, perhaps subconscious, for persons whose avocations centered on creative craftsmanship. That affinity, of course, was consistent with his predisposition to probe for innovative talents when interviewing prospective employees. He was vitally interested in steam locomotives built by Snub Pollard and Jim Goodell, whose basement workshops resembled small manufacturing plants. Pollard spent some six thousand hours over a seven-year period building parts and assembling a five-foot-long engine, tender, and flatcars capable of carrying a dozen persons over a miniature roadbed. Goodell's locomotive, which consumed well over two thousand hours in construction, ran through a wooded area and over a creek alongside his home. He also designed and built gasoline engines, an electricity-producing windmill, and a twenty-six-foot sailboat, the latter a four-year project. John Goodell (younger brother of Jim), who became head of maintenance at Lorain Products in 1971, built a variety of riding mowers of his own design from the parts of abandoned automobiles, and Chuck Scanlan restored antique vehicles. Stocker questioned those men regularly on their progress. "He seemed to sense a special rapport with people who enjoyed putting things together to make something happen," said Scanlan.

Dozens of other employees displayed their workmanship in electronics, mechanics, woodcarving, painting, sketching, sculpture, ceramics, and other crafts at a company hobby show initiated in 1968 by Walter Glick, quality control trainer, and Ray Mercer, a maintenance electrician who also edited the *Sine Wave*. The event proved to be so popular that it became an annual project, growing through the years with the enthusiastic support of the president, who himself excelled at woodworking, including design and construction of fine furniture.

The diversity of Stocker's interests led to so many projects that only his penchant for carefully budgeting time commitments enabled him to pursue them fully enough to satisfy his inquisitiveness. After reading about growing varieties of nuts, he planted black walnut, hickory, and American chestnut trees on land adjoining his Erie County cabin and joined the Northern Nut Growers Association, attending meetings faithfully with Walter Krok, who had a similar interest. Within a short time, he became highly knowledgeable on the subject and fond of observing growth of the new trees on what he referred to as the farm.

Stocker was called on often to head fund drives for charitable causes. "He felt so strongly about supporting worthwhile programs that he was very good at getting others to join in making financial contributions," Nancy recalled. "He never made it a big conversation topic, and he didn't care about receiving credit. When he believed in something that would help people in the community, he simply was willing to contribute time and money to it."

When a capital campaign was launched for a Lorain housing project, City View, Stocker paid for the heating system. "That wasn't a glamorous part of the project," his wife explained, "but Paul said you can't function without those furnaces and pipes, so that's where he wanted to help. He said it would be easier to find donors for the more visible areas of the buildings."

Paul was a member of a board formed to restore and operate a Civic Center that had served as a motion picture theater and gathering place but, like many such bulidings of the 1920s, had been abandoned and left to deteriorate. The magnificent building seated 1,700 persons, and restoration required a continuing fund-raising effort while it was being put back into use for motion pictures, concerts, plays, and myriad other activities, from wrestling to weddings and high school commencements. Beth continued to serve on that board.

Stocker's favorite civic programs were those involving young people and education. He was chairman of the library board for many years until resigning "to get some young blood in there," and he served on the board of Goodwill Industries as well as several other civic boards and committees.

"My husband always said our community and Ohio University had done a lot for us, as well as many other people, and the least we could do was to actively back them," Beth Stocker said. "Our decision to support Ohio University was the feeling that we should help make it possible for young people to have the opportunities we enjoyed at a school we always thought was doing a good job. Paul described it as a way of paying one's dues."

At the request of Dean Robe, Lorain Products—Reliance Comm/Tec in 1985 loaned Stocker's early laboratory models of the Sub-Cycle original patent applications, bound lab notes, and other memorabilia to the Ohio University College of Engineering and Technology, where they were placed on permanent display in the dean's area of Stocker Center.

In that same year, the name of C. Paul Stocker was entered into the Hall of Fame of the Independent Telephone Pioneers Association (ITPA), headquartered in Washington, D.C. Vic Ritter, a member of the Lorain Products sales team, prepared materials for the formal nomination leading to a unanimous election by the organization's Honors Court.

Founded in 1921 as a small group of independent telephone industry members, the ITPA had grown to include 30,000 members with thirty-eight chapters and 149 clubs working "to maintain the principles and pioneering spirit of the industry, while seeking to preserve and promote its history, tradition, and ideals as a contribution to the progress of the nation." Only sixty-six persons had been inducted into its Hall of Fame since the program was started in 1964.

In presenting the posthumous award to Beth Stocker at an October 15, 1985 ceremonial dinner in San Antonio, Honors Court Chairman Wilson B. Garnett spoke of her husband's fourteen "most significant" personal patents, his success as a "manager and valued civic leader," and "his belief in the twin goals of manufacturing only quality products with high reliability, and also maintaining responsible backup services and support . . . while establishing a most enviable record as a manager with special concern for his employees."

A commemorative publication by Lorain Products—Reliance Comm/Tec, in commenting on the award, provided what well could be an epitaph memorializing the career and legacy of C. Paul Stocker:

Founder and driving force behind Lorain Products for nearly forty years, Mr. Stocker was one of the few manufacturing executives to receive this distinction.

And although he considered himself an engineer and wasn't much taken with honors, he would have been proud of this one.

He was a telephone man, first and last, and he built his company with the sole objective of serving the telephone industry. And now, fifty years later, Lorain Products is still guided by that principle.

This philosophy of service carried through Mr. Stocker's private life, as well. He worked as hard and as selflessly for his community; he was a leader in local service activities as well as professional engineering organizations.

Mr. Stocker's humanity, vision, and integrity are his legacy. We're proud to be his heirs.

DOCUMENTATION

Although much of the information for this book was gleaned from interviews, letters, and individual memoirs, specifics, including dates and figures, were found in such documents as company memoranda, newspapers, magazines, brochures, news releases, catalogs, annual reports, minutes of board meetings, courthouse records, and a wide variety of personal notes and other materials from company archives. Information was cross-checked among these various sources whenever possible. Most sources are cited within the text or made obvious by their content. The following listing refers only to information that warrants further specific documentation.

CHAPTER ONE

General information on the United States at the turn of the century is documented in the *Encyclopedia of American History*, (Harper & Row); *The History of the Telephone*, by Herbert N. Casson (A. C. McClurg & Co., 1918); and selected volumes of *Scientific American, Outlook,* and *Scribner's* magazines. Material on Tuscarawas County was gleaned from newspapers and historical records in libraries. Stocker family information came from interviews, newspapers, letters, and a genealogy report prepared through extensive research by members of the family.

CHAPTER TWO

Information concerning Ohio University was taken from *The History of Ohio University*, by Thomas Nathanael Hoover (The Ohio University Press, 1954) and from a condensed version of *The History of Engineering at Ohio*

University, by Dr. Reuben M. Olson. Material for the profile of New York City in 1926 was researched in copies of New York newspapers and encyclopedias. Segments of the information on telephones, Bell Laboratories, and the Bell System were gleaned from "The History of Engineering and Science in the Bell System."

CHAPTER THREE

Lorain County history was researched in newspapers, booklets, and pamphlets in the Lorain County Library and in a revised edition of "The Story of Lorain: An International City," published in 1985 by the Lorain City School District. Data on the telephone industry during the Great Depression was found in articles appearing in the January 1935 and October 1936 issues of *Southern Telephone News*. Company products were explained in Lorain Products records and in an article by Paul Stocker.

CHAPTER FOUR

The state of the U. S. economy and the telephone industry in the late 1930s, which served as an introduction and general background for the entire chapter, was researched in *Business Week, Fortune, New Republic*, and *Telephony* magazines, and the *Wall Street Journal*. Figures on defense appropriation in the early 1940s were contained in the First Quarterly Report, for period ending April 30, 1942, of the U. S. Office of Price Administration. General information of that period was found in newspapers and *The Economic History of the United States*, volume 9, by Broadus Mitchell (Rinehart & Co.). All other information came from interviews, and from letters and reports written by former employees of Lorain Products.

CHAPTER FIVE

The state of American business, industry, government, and

military affairs during and immediately following World War II was researched in *The History of American Business and Industry*, by Alex Groner and the editors of *American Heritage* and in *Business Week, Fortune, Time*, and *Newsweek* magazines and the *Encyclopedia of American History*, bicentennial edition, edited by Richard B. Morris (Harper & Row).

CHAPTER SIX

General information on the telephone industry was gleaned from newspapers, several issues of *Southern Telephone News*, and "The Spirit of Independent Telephony," by Charles A. Pleasance (Independent Telephone Books, 1989). Reports on the Lorain Products fire were found in the *Lorain Journal*, the *Cleveland Plain Dealer*, and the *Cleveland Press*. Information on the Ohio University sesquicentennial and involvement by the Stockers was contained in December 1953 and April 1956 issues of the *Ohio Alumnus* magazine.

CHAPTER SEVEN

The business climate of the United States in the late 1950s was researched in *Business Week* and *Nation's Business* from 1957 through 1959. Data on telephone companies was reported in *Business Week* and the *New York Times Magazine*. All other information for chapter 7 was obtained from interviews, company records, reports, official documents, and letters.

CHAPTER EIGHT

The state of America's economy in 1959 was summarized from research in *Business Week, Fortune, Nation's Business*, and *Vital Speeches of the Times*. Information on construction in Canada was contained in the *Lorain Journal*, the *St. Thomas Times-Journal*, letters, and company records.

CHAPTER NINE

General material on Sputnik and its impact on American education was gathered from various issues of the *New York Times, Vital Speeches of the Times,* and publications of educational organizations. Activities of Ohio's Commission on Education beyond the High School and plans during the early Alden administration were reported n the *Ohio Alumnus* magazine. Information on Paul Stocker's association with Ohio University was obtained from files of the university and its College of Engineering and Technology, as well as from numerous interviews.

CHAPTER TEN

All information for this chapter was obtained from company resources, interviews, and personal communications by Paul Stocker.

CHAPTER ELEVEN

Economic repercussions of the war in Vietnam were gleaned from reports in various U. S. magazines and newspapers of the 1960s.

CHAPTER TWELVE

Research materials for Mexico's political, economic, and industrial development in the late 1960s included speech transcriptions in the *Department of State Bulletin* (November 20, 1967; March 4, 1968); *U. S. News and World Report* (June 4, 1967; October 2, 1967; July 1, 1968); *Time* (October 13, 1967; November 3, 1967); *Business Week* (June 24, 1967); and *Newsweek* (August 7, 1967). Biographic information on Noel Trainor supplementing that contained in company files, was gleaned from a May 22, 1970 article in the *Mexico City News.*

CHAPTER THIRTEEN

All resource information for this chapter came from documents of the merger of Lorain Products and Reliance Electric, and from personal interviews.

CHAPTER FOURTEEN

Reports of the breakup of AT&T were found in *Newsweek, Business Week, Forbes, Time,* and *U. S. News and World Report.*

CHAPTER FIFTEEN

Information presented in this chapter is documented within the text.

CHAPTER SIXTEEN

Information concerning the Independent Telephone Pioneer Association and its Hall of Fame was provided by the IPTA, Washington, D. C.

INDEX

A NOTE ABOUT THE AUTHOR

A graduate of Ohio University, David Neal Keller was a newspaperman and industrial writer before returning to his alma mater for ten years as director of public relations and editor of alumni publications. Since 1967 he has been a full time freelance writer and filmmaker. He has written and produced more than a hundred sponsored films and videotapes, and his byline has appeared on a variety of magazine articles. This is his third book. Mr. Keller and his wife, Marian, who live at Keowee Key in South Carolina, have three married children and seven grandchildren.